POLICE ENFORCEMENT CRIMES AND INJUSTICES

POLICE ENFORCEMENT CRIMES AND INJUSTICES

James Vadackumchery

GYAN PUBLISHING HOUSE
NEW DELHI-110 002

POLICE ENFORCEMENT CRIMES AND INJUSTICES
Criminology, Public Administration, Police, Law

ISBN: 81-212-0721-5

Published in 2001 in India by
Gyan Publishing House
5, Ansari Road,
New Delhi-110 002
Phone: 3282060, 3261060, Fax: 3285914
E-mail: gyanbook@del2.vsnl.net.in
Visit Our Web Site At http:\\www.gyanbooks.com

Laser Typesetting at: Power Photocomposers, New Delhi-110 002.
Printed at: Mehra Offset Press, New Delhi-110002.

Contents

Preface

Today, entering the third millennium, one sees only computers in India. As a result, a new generation of management experts comes into being. They want to speed up the process in all areas of human activities—including law enforcement. Now, as it is, there is undue delay at each and every stage in administration of justice. Delay is seen in investigation, in prosecution, in trial, and in what not, so much so, that a criminal case is disposed off after several years—even decades if appeals are filed. Everyone knows the objectives of punishment from deterrent or retributive theories to correction and reformation of criminals and crime-doers. If correction of the offender and his reformation are aimed at, then there is no justification in causing undue delay in initiating the corrective and reformative processes. No doubt, the police, prosecutors, courts and corrections show their inability to define their missions resulting in miscarriage of justice—resulting in the commission of a variety of enforcement crimes. In my earlier books, I have discussed in detail what I meant by enforcement crimes and enforcement justice/injustice. From what is seen today, any one may think that there is goal misunderstanding among the various agencies involved in administering justice. The book—*'The Police, Enforcement Crimes and* Injustice deals only with police, a sub-system tha investigates and prevents crimes.

"The courts handcuff the police"—I have heard this for the last two decades from police officers/men.

"The press handcuffs the police"— some police officers say so. "The people handcuff the police"

"The laws handcuff the police",

"The human rights activists handcuff the police"

"The departmental superiors handcuff the subordinate police officers",

"The politicians handcuff the police"— and thus the police

functionaries say that a situation has come into being that they cannot function effectively, honestly, independently and with sincerity. The police are fettered everywhere and precisely therefore, there exists a system of Check and Balance as various agencies exert too much control and power on police functionings. Is it true to think so?

The courts today are forced to intervene in many things police do. The Supreme Court in *D.K. Basu Vs. State of West Bengal* has given a directive to the police that custody/arrest memo must be issued to people when they are taken into custody/arrested. The magistrates verify it when the suspect is produced before the Court. In the Code of Criminal Procedure—1973, there are a number of provisions which are enacted to ensure detinue—justice and the courts verify whether or not the suspects, arrestees, detainees are dealt with as per law and the procedure established by law. The procedures make it clear that there can take place, violations of law in police stations or when the suspects, arrestees or detinues are in police custody. The Indian laws attest to the fact that there exist enforcement crimes. Provisions are seen in the Indian Penal Code to punish custodial torture and the Indian Evidence Act make confessions to police officers inadmissible and in their presence Human Rights Commissions award heavy compensation to the victims of abuse of power/authority by police. What do they indicate? They show that enforcement crimes are in vogue while crimes are investigated by police. Can the computers and software associated with automatic processings help to reduce enforcement crimes? As far as law enforcement system is concerned, doubtlessly, it is large multifaceted and is intended to control human behaviour. The police are expected to apprehend offenders and treat them in a human rights friendly way. But, the allegation is that they fail to or refuse to do so. The result is that enforcement crimes do take place during police work.

Can the police perform their functions/mission without violating laws? Opinions differ as some say that police work contains violation of laws in some way or other. According to them, law enforcement without law violations may be an utopian idea and as such, enforcement crimes are necessary evils in justice administration. People, therefore, have to bear this fact in mind when they speak about police and crimes. Not withstanding the argument posed above, people in a democracy think that they have a right to demand law enforcement through law observation (and not by law violation) and the police have a duty to offer such a violation-free law enforcement.

Individual success and organizational achievements—they are two aspects of police work. Enforcement crimes may, sometimes, ensure individual success in police work. The officer may be called efficient, intelligent, capable, outstanding, etc., and I know a number of police officers/men who are honoured thus by the police and the people. The people may demand the services of such law enforcement officers to achieve their targets, for they want only success in their cases, but, in due course—-after some time-they themselves may criticize the police officers/men who enforce law through law violations or enforcement crimes. Experience and history so far reveals that law enforcement through law violations do not ensure organizational achievements. The image of the organization is tarnished and the individuals who make the organization are caricatured in bad shape when they commit enforcement crimes. It goes, therefore, without saying that an individuals success is accomplished only when the organization's success is guaranteed. May be that the individuals who constitute the organization are ignorant of this reality—so much so that they involve themselves in committing enforcement crimes thinking that the success in their work through unacceptable means is the success of the organization they represent. Some become emotional to the extent of becoming irrational while some others become rational to the extent of becoming emotional. In both situations, the result is the commission of enforcement crimes which in the long run defeats the success of the organization. Law enforcement is a process of enforcing law and in doing so, the decisions and actions, affect the future of the organization in a rational manner and in a way desired by the people in a democracy—in a way as per law and procedure established by law. Desired by the people, law and procedure established by law is of paramount significance in a democracy.

Problems may come up during law enforcement and crime investigation and they help to find out means and methods to solve the problems—in a just and people friendly manner. No problem or dilemma is easily resolved or if at all resolved, new and different kinds of problems and dilemmas may come up. Commission of enforcement crimes to solve the problems/dilemmas is not a solution to the issues, but is a problem that damages the reputation of the police department. A police service which does not recognize the "society's needs" can not survive during the next century. What values, what philosophies, what goals, what needs, what strategies—all these become significantly important in police work today. Becoming insensitive to such "What" will have its undeniable consequences during the years to come. The end in itself will not glorify police activities and functionings-rather-the methods used to achieve the end matter a lot. The police have been doing a lot of good things in the past. The question here is: "Did they work well so that the people appreciated the work which the police had been doing till date?".

The police department is not a business organization—is not a corporation—is not a company. It is a community of people intended to deal with and control people and their behaviour. Everything the police perform have lasting implications on the lives of many in society. This is the precise reason why enforcement crimes are disfavoured by the people and law. Police need policy planning and programme planning. Do the police have a "Policy"?. If there is a 'policy' for the police, then the programmes can be planned accordingly. I, for one, think that the police have been experimenting with programmes and they wanted to see whether or not they worked well. Thus the failure in police work came about and it was one of the main reasons why enforcement crimes took place during police work. Remember always that the police deal with people—people of all categories and descriptions and not with stocks and machines. Hence any programme without a well defined and thought-out plan cannot yield good dividends. Evaluation research in a scientific way on police activities and performance was unheard in police and therefore was of little or no significance in police performance. What is the most effective, efficient, valuable, result-ensuring, desirable strategy to ensure human rights friendly and enforcement crime-free policing has never attracted much attention in society. People who talk a lot against police are also not very keen to improve the police. Many politicians who make noise in the legislatures/Parliament are not meaning anything seriously when they vacate the platforms inside and outside the leglsiature/Parliament. A good many among them are inclined to use and misuse the police machinery for their selfish interests. In order to please the politicians, some police officers commit enforcement crimes.

Can the society think about establishing enforcement crime-free atmosphere? For, enforcement crime implies injustice or miscarriage of justice. A traditional criminological approach to the question of finding the causes of enforcement criminality may be many which include: (1) to get quick result, (2) to make easy money, (3) to obtain individual glory, fame and success, (4) to please certain people who are powerful or influential, (5) to show retribution or vengeance (6) to exhibit power and authority, (7) to make fortune or privileges and many such factors. Of course, all of them may directly or indirectly have an influencing component to commit enforcement crimes, and any one of them by itself may not be the sole cause of enforcement crimes. Perhaps a multiple causation approach may better explain the etiological factors of enforcement crimes. The speciality of enforcement crimes is that the crime doers commit crimes and live in society as if they were law abiding citizens whose sole aim in the job is to protect the people and society from crime and criminals. Very little, if any, attention has been paid so far to understand the etiology, extent and intensity of enforcement crimes in police department. If at all any inquiry is conducted, it is just to investigate a crime by an enforcement functionary provided some one prefers a complaint against such a functionary. Otherwise, everything happening is taken for granted and no meaningful research is conducted in this special area of criminological importance. Enforcement crimes assume a lot of importance in current criminological researches. The reason is that the damage caused to the police department today by the enforcement criminals is so high that the people lose their trust and confidence in just and fair law enforcement and crime investigation.

* A constable enters a theatre without purchasing a ticket.
* A head constable dishonestly tells that the fuel allowed for the month is exhausted.
* An assistant sub-inspector asks a motor vehicle driver to hand over the licence for over speeding the vehicle. He takes the licence to his possession.
* A sub-inspector keeps a juvenile offender under police custody.
* A circle inspector gets his motor vehicle repaired free of cost.
* A deputy superintendent of police receives regular pay—off from liquor dealers.
* A superintendent of police becomes susceptible to political influence. And thus one may identify a variety of areas of enforcement criminality.

In one of my earlier books, I have brought out the fact that enforcement crimes could be seen in all branches of *law* enforcement. They could be seen in income tax, sale tax, forest, excise, customs, railways, panchayat and municipalities, etc., However, this book does not discuss enforcement crimes in all government departments. It confines only to the police department as often the criticisms against the police quite upset me. People always say that the behaviour of the policemen/officers must be above reproach. Police ethics must be a part of police training curriculum and the department must find out ways and methods to discipline the unethical conducts of police functionaries. Enforcement criminality should not have any place in police work. Every police officer/man has a duty to his department, to the people and to the society. In a very few instances, these duties may conflict one another and in such situations, the rule is:

"Do the right thing according to one's conscience" under the given circumstances. Parade ground discipline may be good to do many things in police—but can never be a substitute for an upright human conscience. An upright conscience says that a police officer/man has a duty to his profession/job and the job/profession is not to commit enforcement crimes for enforcing law and justice. People want responsible policing and in enforcing professional responsibility, there is no scope for any enforcement criminality. Do things as per law—as per the procedure established by law—as per an upright human conscience—as per human rights friendly principles—and if possible, it is desirable to employ a "good faith" test whenever things are not clear.

In any and every enforcement, an ethical issue is also involved. A police officer must see, beyond and besides law, the ethics of police acts. Of course, the law protects a police officer—and ethics protects his human conscience. For, ethics deals with the manner in which the law has been enforced. In ethical law enforcement, both means and ends are justified. In such a situation, enforcement crimes do not come into being. It is against law to commit a murder, but it is also against law to cause custodial murder in order to prove the crime committed by the murderer.

Police are but one sub-system in the justice system, but their visibility conspicuously exceeds that of all other sub-systems. Precisely, therefore, the enforcement crimes committed by police become a topic of discussion for many. People, as a whole, do not see prosecutors, judges and correctional personnel whereas they do see and experience the police every day. As such, an enforcement crime committed by police may be seen in day light and discussed in loud voice by the people.

Law enforcement and enforcement of law may mean one and the samething. Enforcement crime and enforcement of crime may mean entirely different things. Enforcement crimes—like white collar crimes—may be described as crimes (law violations) by an enforcement personnel during the course of law enforcement. The objective may be anything from ego inflation to monetary gains. While committing enforcement crimes, there may be not only violations of the penal laws, but also violations of ethical, social, cultural, behavioural, religious and other laws. Law enforcement officers/men admit that they violate laws, but they bring several interpretations and justifications for their otherwise illegal acts. Enforcement crimes, as indicated earlier, are not confined to police department. They are seen in all departments in varying ways, numbers and measures.

Police officers/men bring out their occupational demands as necessary element for committing enforcement crimes. They argue that so long as the occupational demands are not neutralized, it is hypothesized that enforcement crimes will continue to be committed by police functionaries. No, there are other reasons too for committing enforcement crimes by police. My researches and observations reveal that any individual who opts for police job will in due course become insensitive, authoritarian, cynical, aliented, dogmatic, unsympathetic, inhuman or even anomic and the position may be different in other countries where the culture and values are different. In India, today, suicides of police personnel are on the increase. Why? Is it because there exists depression among police functionaries? Likewise, suicides of detinues in police custody are on the increase. Why? Is it because, the detainees too are equally depressed as the police personnel. Anyway, the questions are more and the answers are limited and partial. When a suspect in a burglary was questioned, the police resorted to third degree methods until atlast he died in police custody. Certainly, an enforcement crime has been committed by the enforcement officers/men. Why did the police employ third degree methods? The readymade answer to the question might be that the deadly force was employed to get a confession from the suspect. The next questions would be: "What is the duty of a police officer/man first? Is it to protect human life—or to protect the private property of the victim of burglary?". Why does police employ deadly force to protect property more than to protect human lives?" and the questions thus are many.

These are the times of police accountability for everything they do or commit. Enforcement criminality comes within the purview of police accountability. People ask questions and the police have to answer them. The chapters that follow comment on several aspects of enforcement crimes in police. Chapter 1 is all about enforcement crimes in police service. The extent and intensity of enforcement crimes in police, the etiology of such crimes and characteristics of enforcement criminals are discussed. In Chapter 2, the origin, development and persistence of enforcement crimes have been brought out. Police must know that times have changed now and they can no longer consider themselves as the coercive weapon of the Government in power. They are public servants and their patrons are the people in a democracy. Chapter 3, is about recruitment, training and enforcement crimes. Acquittals and convictions in criminal cases are not free from enforcement crimes. The undercurrents in acquittals and convictions may be the enforcement crimes committed by the sub-systems in justice administration. This is discussed in Chapter 4. Chapter 5, is all about delay in investigation and disposal of cases. The inordinate delay is a curse and the victims of delayed disposal are condemned to suffer the consequences.

Discipline and disciplinary justice are areas where one can notice a variety of enforcement crimes. Crimes committed by the higher ups in the hierarchy—the helpless and the voiceless mortals suffer the ill effects of such enforcement crimes. Chapter 6 deals with the issue elaborately.

Human formation, intellectual formation, physical training, legal and ethical formation, etc, are discussed in many fora in these days. There is an identity crisis in police and this is more so when the people have high expectations. Equal justice system—a system that offers distributive justice to the criminals, to the victims, to the victims of abuse of power and authority, to the society and to the system itself may offer solutions to the burning issues and they are treated in Chapter 7.

Human Contents and Human Elements—they are two important ingredients in law enforcements and justice administration. Man initiates action against man and makes judgements against himself and others. There is the importance and relevance of human element in police actions. Man is human and he ought to be human in his attitudes and approaches and there comes the human content in police transactions. Any police action devoid of human contents and human elements will be disfavoured by humanity. Police must obey the laws—human and statutory-more than his own law for enforcing laws for others. Being so, a police officer must, in his activity, separate his individual, personal and private conscience from that of public human conscience and try to enforce the law as the people want it to be enforced. There is the need to discover the basic human elements and human contents in law enforcement. In no sphere of police activities can one's personal whims take the place of his conscience or dictate norms concerning things which are outside his personal whims, which are of ensuring just justice to people through the recognition and defence of their human rights. Precisely therefore, police strategies must ensure that all people enjoy respect for their human person and dignity. Any act which rejects the acceptance of human rights to people will cause more serious harm to all including those who work in law eforcment. Police have the duty to protect people against abuses which may occur while they enforce law in society.

Enforcement crimes are thus crimes which no law can claim

to legitimize. If any one in police—be he the director general of police or the bottom most police constable—commits an enforcement crime, there is no obligation for others to obey such a person in authority, instead there is a grave and clear obligation to oppose them aggressively by conscientious objections. The Police Acts clearly lay down the law that police officers are to obey only the lawful orders of their superiors. In every day functionings of police, some conscientious people show resistance to the unjust commands of those in authority and in so doing they show their strength in not committing enforcement crimes even in compelling circumstances.

This book—*Police, Enforcement Crimes and Injustices*—throws lights on various types of enforcement crimes that take place in police service. Police officers are called upon under grave obligation of their conscience not to co-operate willfully in practices which, even if encouraged or appreciated, are enforcement crime prone in their work. Let this thought guide the police functionaries in the years to come.

I have received a lot of assistance from my wife, Mary and daughters, Neethu and Neethie. They wholeheartedly enlightened me with their opinions and visions about enforcement crimes that take place in other government departments. Their services are gratefully acknowledged and I say a "thank you" to each one of them.

The views and opinions expressed in this book are personal and are derived from my observations and researches. They do not reflect the views and opinions of the Government of India, State Governments, Police Departments and Home Offices.

Thiruvananthapuram, Crmgst Dr. James Vadackumchery
2000

1
NATURE AND EXTENT

Enforce means 'compel obedience to' and enforcement of law means 'compel obedience to law'. Enforcement Crime means a crime committed by the enforcement machinery while the law is enforced. While enforcing law, the police may be charged with ineptness, partiality, discourtesy, indecency, dishonesty, cruelty, brutality, indifference, sleeping on duty, lethargy, illegal searches, informal arrests, calling of epithets, unnecessary detentions, concoction of evidence, perfunctory investigation, human rights unfriendly approaches, etc. The police may be attacked by the people, press, courts as being insensitive to the feelings and needs of citizens they are employed to serve. The result is that there is not a smooth functioning of the police system. People see that the laws are violated when the law is enforced. This sort of law violation is called an enforcement crime in current criminology.

As per law, the police alone are empowered to do certain things and the police do not do so, it means that they are violating the law. Police alone can investigate a crime and they alone can register a first information report. If they do not do so, then what can be done? The police alone can investigate a crime and they cause long delay for completion of investigation, then what can be done? Police alone can inspect a scene of crime and collect evidence. If they do not do so or collect evidence or collect evidence in a contaminated way, then what can be done? If the police arrest wrong persons or effect arrests of real culprits and keep them in police custody incommunicado for many days, then what can be done?

The people and the police know that the police in such situations violate the provisions in the Code of Criminal Procedure-1973. Nevertheless, what can be done? There may be remedies or reliefs, but it becomes indeed very difficult and financially unbearable for ordinary citizens to get a legal remedy for the injustice committed on them who are generally poor and are not influential otherwise.

Enforcement Crimes—Extent and Intensity

Once a police officer said: "It is impossible to get a conviction unless the investigator manipulates some records. Honestly investigated criminal cases may end in acquittals, whereas criminal cases with concocted evidence, created witnesses and manipulated records may get an easier conviction than an honest case". Although this is an exaggerated version, one may see a lot of truth in that statement. For, it seems that enforcement crimes are a *sine qua non* for conviction of criminal cases from Indian courts. People have right to be secure in their persons, houses, papers and effects against unreasonable searches and seizures. Nevertheless, persons are searched during odd hours of the night at their houses without showing decency to the privacy of the family members. If this is done, it is doubtlessly a misuse of authority and to that extent is an enforcement crime and a human right violation. No person shall be compelled in any criminal case to be a witness against himself. This is otherwise called protection against self-incriminatory evidence. In a reported case[1], the police illegally broke into the privacy of a person and found him consuming two capsules containing morphine. Police took him to the hospital where a doctor forced an emetic solution through a tube into his stomach, causing him to vomit. It was held by the court that "this course of proceeding by agents of government to obtain evidence is bound to offend even hardened sensibilities". This is, therefore, nothing but enforcement crime by government agencies to which the citizen had no option other than to yield.

In *D.K. Basu Vs. State of West Bengal*, the Supreme Court of India has given the directive that a counsel could be present when the suspect was interrogated. Of course, the Court did not allow the counsel to be present all throughout the interrogation. A police interrogator, thereafter, allowed the counsel to be present during interrogation. He was allowed to sit at a distance and in such a way that he could see only the back of the interrogated. The counsel later complained that the behaviour of the police interrogator was an enforcement crime.

Thus, one may see any number of enforcement crimes which law enforcement officers commit during the course of an investigation. Police are legally bound to maintain law and order, investigate and prevent crimes, protect life and property, honour human rights and individual freedom. But, it may be seen that violations do take place in many ways and all these violations can be rightly called enforcement crimes.

'Enforcement crime' is not defined anywhere—except in my book—and therefore, it is not possible to locate my judgements about enforcement crimes by police. Nevertheless, a number of criminal cases were acquitted because the courts observed some form of enforcement crimes. A few judgments are quoted under—

* "The F.I.R. was made by the father of the deceased to whom all the important facts of the occurrence was bound to have been communicated. But, in the F.I.R., it was not mentioned that appellant had stabled the deceased. The omission of such an important fact is relevant under S.11 of the Evidence Act in judging the veracity of the prosecution".[2]
* This was a clear case of enforcement criminality. A veteran police investigator who was in charge of a police station prepared the F.I.R. and in so doing, he omitted very important facts. The informant was not aware of the requirements in a F.I.R. and the rule was that the investigating officer ought to have questioned the informant before recording the same. Ignorance of how to question a first informant, in a way, resulted in the acquittal of the case from the Supreme Court of India.

How much money, manpower and time would be wasted for the people, exchequer and the Government whenever cases were acquitted by the Courts. On the other side, how much expenditure, manpower and time was expended by the accused in crime? All these originated from the enforcement crime committed by the officer who prepared the F.I.R.

* "A police officer should not insist that a woman should appear at the police station, as this contravenes Section 160 (1)".[3] No doubt, police officers call women to police stations in many instances and the women, being afraid of the evil consequences go to police stations. This is a violation of law and on that count alone, it is an enforcement crime. The police are accountable for the crime they commit and to that extent, the police are liable to pay compensation to the victim of the misuse of police authority/power.

* "If the police record becomes suspect or unreliable on the ground that it was deliberately perfunctory or dishonest, it loses much of its value".[4] The observation made by the Supreme Court made it clear that enforcement crimes committed by police became a ground for causing suspicion about the truthfulness of the police records. Necessarily, it caused heavy loss to the public exchequer and therefore it should have been realized from the police officers responsible for committing crimes. As the concept of 'enforcement crime' is of recent origin and the principle of realizing compensation caused to public money entrusted to the government are of later origin, there is a school of thought which argues that conviction rate can be improved if the investigating officers are given liability for miscarriage of justice through their enforcement crimes.

* "The injuries shown in the Inquest Report and the post mortem report do not tally".[5] Why? Was it not an enforcement criminality? Thus, one may see any number of enforcement crimes in every stage of investigation. The defence counsels

take note of these loopholes to get aquittal verdicts in criminal cases.

Enforcement Crimes: Why?

Mistake of law, mistake of fact, done in good faith, done for the greater welfare of the society, done without any malicious intention, done during official work—all these phrases and cliche-ridden expressions have been used to mitigate the seriousness of police misdoings. No one thought about enforcement crimes as the police had a lot of immunity when they did many things against law and procedure established by law.

* Police used to take people in custody without making any record of the same. Certainly, it was an enforcement crime, nevertheless, neither the police nor the people treated it to be an enforcement crime. There is a limit to human tolerance and as such, the Supreme Court of India now insists that the police must issue a custody/arrest memo to any one who is taken into custody/arrested by police. People now approach Human Rights Commissions claiming compensation for subjecting them to informal/illegal arrests by police. If and when human rights courts start functioning, the informal/illegal arrests which the police make will be treated as a human rights violation or enforcement crimes for which they will be made liable to pay compensation to the victims of the abuse of power/authority.

The governments/police departments do not and cannot own the responsibility for enforcement crimes which police officers commit during law enforcement. The arguments are that: (1) The police officers are appointed to enforce law in a lawful manner; (2) They are not even remotely thought to involve in illegalities; (3) If they do unlawful acts during law enforcement, the responsibility is theirs and not of the police departments or governments; (4) Police officers/men responsible for law violations will pay the damages. Hence, a departmental inquiry is conducted to fix the responsibility of enforcement crimes.

The Push and Pull Factors

Why do the police commit enforcement crimes? A study was conducted to identify the causes of enforcement crimes and altogether, 87 causes could be identified. Out of them some—17 in all-were isolated and they were—

1. False ego feelings and pseudo—authoritarianism.
2. Desire to make easy money by quick means.
3. Quest for occupying certain posts/positions for a longer period.
4. Vulnerability/susceptibility, political influence and godfatherly treatments.
5. Urge to have quick result by short—cut methods.
6. Longing for name, fame, success and achievements.
7. Ignorance about the laws, rules, procedures and code of conduct.
8. Lack of information about police ethics, professionalism, expertise, etc.
9. Defective formation of an upright conscience, superego concepts and moral code.
10. Over-effect of "id" complexes (Freud), animal energies, instincts.
11. Loss of self-esteem, human conscience and legal-mindness.
12. False notions about law enforcement and administration of justice.
13. Effect of defective personality development, psychopathy and psychic disorders to do certain things without guilt feelings.

14. Neglect of equity, good conscience and principles of natural justice to the victims of the abuse of power and authority.

15. Subjective interpretation of objectively objectionable acts and deriving of mental satisfaction through rational and justifications.

16. Ethical relativism which make some to think that they are always right even when they commit legal wrongs.

17. Inclination to commit cruel or illegal acts in the name of truth, social welfare, human happiness and administration of justice.

All the factors enumerated above are push *factors* for enforcement criminality. They work within an individual as they are having more of psychological contents. Besides and beyond the subjective elements, there are many factors which work as pull *factors* and the study brought out 41 such factors. The most important ones are listed below:-

1. Culture and police sub-culture which promote enforcement criminality.

2. Silent approval and open encouragement by supervisory ranks for enforcement criminality provided it produces quick results.

3. Laws and rules which favour enforcement criminality. They give immunity to the enforcement crime-doers for the acts they commit even in the wrong way.

4. Public's tolerance and indifferents to enforcement crimes. Sometimes, they encourage enforcement crimes.

5. Political pressure and pressure from upstairs in police edifice.

6. Influence of money and other favours.

7. Social processes such as imitation, identification and suggestion, etc.

8. Facilitating environments and stimulating atmosphere.

Police is a sub-system in justice administration and as such it is only a means and not an end. Its value depends upon its conformity to justice-just justice. Its justness depends upon the justness of the ends which it pursues and of the means it employs. Enforcement criminality can not be accepted as a just means to reach a just end—i.e., administration of justice and ensuring of social welfare. The value of the responsible police system stands or falls with the values which it embodies and promotes. Values such as just justice through just means for the "Common Good" of the society are certainly fundamental for the existence and survival of any police system in a democracy.

Enforcement Crimes and Police Image

Whatever may be the causes of enforcement crimes and the rationale for their justifications, enforcement crimes and criminals tarnish the police image—even among school—going children. For several decades, enforcement criminality has been in vogue in India and if the same trend continues in the years to come, the police system itself will be shaken in its foundations and will be forcefully converted to function as a service which respects human rights and the dignity of every human person, etc.

What did the police achieve so far by their acts and activities for their image building? Police are doing enviable service to the people, but they do not get a name and image for the service they render to the people. Why? One of the main reasons for a low profile and an unenviable image is found to be the enforcement criminality which is seen practised in police sub-culture. There is a lot of literature on this and it can be seen in the reports of police commissions, judgements of the courts of law and research studies by scholars. They do not see them as "enforcement crimes" rather, they view them as undesirable strategies in police sub-culture.

Characteristics of an Enforcement Criminal

Unlike a pickpocket, a thief, a murderer, an enforcement criminal does not think that he is a criminal indeed. Instead, he thinks that he is administering justice. An enforcement criminal is often a psychopath who does not have any guilt feeling for the illegality he does. He delays the proceedings, receives money, harasses people, victimizes them and he has a justification for everything he does.

An enforcement criminal is selfish. More than that, one may see 'selfism' in him. Selfism, according to me is selfishness which harms others. In selfishness, there may not be any harm to other people whereas in selfism, there is. Enforcement criminals suffer from defective personality development and moral consciousness. Their super-ego (Freud) is inadequately formed.

He interprets sometimes his capacity to commit enforcement crimes as his efficiency. He thinks too much about himself and likes to boost himslef. He behaves as if he were the law. He interprets law to his advantage. He misuses his position an makes an earning by his otherwise criminal activities

He decides on many things or has accessibility to people who take decisions. He has no accountability for what he does and therefore he has a protective umbrella. He believes that any justice done is a charity done to the people. He is not bound by time or other forces. He finds excuses for everything he does and feels immune from any responsibility over the acts/omissions he does.

An enforcement criminal has foul motives although he appears to be a different person. His source traits are different from his surface traits. He is insensitive, inept, easily susceptible to irritation, insincere, dishonest and incapable to honour human emotions and sentiments. He has no respect to human dignity and individual freedom. He is an 'island' and has no altruist sentiments. He considers his position more than human values. He is hypersensitive and may do anything to harm others. He may concoct evidence to see that an accused is punished in a criminal case.

An enforcement criminal has no self-esteem. He treats others as "nobody"; nevertheless, is very much afraid of political power and authority. He is vulnerable to influences/introductions as he is afraid of evil consequences from such forces. He knows that he manages and manipulates things to his advantage and therefore, he shows an excessive fear to power and authority which can harm him. He has an uneasiness in him as he is fearful of many things/many people.

He speaks about many good things he has done to others and he does so just to cover the ill-doings he has done. He wants to convince himself that he is doing the right thing, but he cannot as he knows that he is not doing the right thing. He is a moral wreck and has only a weak ethical ego. He blames many people and things for his ill-doings. He wants to justify his acts and likes to rationalize his doings. He fails often and therefore he may find consolation in drinks, drugs, prayers, spirituality, etc. He becomes mentally disturbed at times and becomes neurotic in extreme cases.

Enforcement crimes and enforcement criminals are not treated as they are in their real nature. Therefore, the enforcement criminals do not feel that they are committing crimes when they do so. Any criminal law does not define enforcement crimes and prescribes punishments for them. As such, people do not think that there is a special category of crimes called enforcement crimes. While bribery, corruption, etc., are considered as crimes, no one treats bureaucratic hoarding of files as a crime which may be punished. Delay in the disposal of files causes miscarriage of justice and is very much an enforcement crime.

* In one instance, police officers simply refused to arrest the culprit in spite of convincing evidence. The reason was that they were influenced by the political forces. People, ultimately conducted *dharnas*, processions, street corner meetings and hunger strikes to pressure the authorities to take actions against the culprit. It means that the

people and the media now come forward to fight against enforcement crimes. Nevertheless, there is no law to initiate action against the enforcement criminal now. At the most some disciplinary actions may be initiated and most of them have a natural death. There is no accountability for the enforcement crimes committed and consequently, there is no criminal liability for them. The enforcement criminals are a protected lot and they enjoy immunity for many things they do in the name of justice or in the pretext of administering justice.

* In a Gulf country, I am told by my brother Osborn that the police put one note of high denomination in a public place and watch whether or not it is being taken by someone. In case the police notice that the note is taken possession of by someone, they catch hold of him/her and initiate criminal proceedings. Subsequently, he/she is punished. I asked him: "What is it?". Giving temptation for people to commit crimes and then punish them for the crimes they commit is not administration of justice, rather it is an enforcement crime. Man is not always the master of all situations. He is fragile and any law enforcement officer may become vulnernable to temptations if the temptations persist on him. In a South Indian State, once, some young and lovely police women dressed beautifully went to bus stations, railway platforms and started giving signals signifying their inclination to become subjects of eve-teasing. Young boys fell prey to their soliciting and provoking signals and invitations. Immediately, policemen in mufty caught hold of them for *eve-teasing* and the news appeared in the media. Is it administration of justice? Is it not misuse of authority? Is it not an enforcement crime to do so?. There are more questions than answers to such enforcement criminality. Victimologists may subscribe to the view that a law enforcement officer too can be tempted to behave like an eve-teaser in similar situations.

Enforcement crimes are numerous and an honest answer to the questions: "what are the various ways the police misuse their power and authority or what are the crooked ways of behaviour in police functions?" will give the extent and intensity of enforcement crimes.

I took the daily newspapers for 10 months and wanted to see the number of private complaints filed against police. I could see that there were a number of private complaints preferred against the police on many counts and certainly, they indicate a portion of the prevailing enforcement crimes in police department. Some such published crimes were:

* Women were kept in illegal custody for several hours in police stations.
* Children whose age is below 16 years, if male, were shown as 18 in order to proceed against them as adult offenders. The Juvenile Justice Act—1986 says that male children under 16 years of age and female children under 18 years of age must be treated as per the provisions contained in the Juvenile Justice Act—1986. Raising the age up helps the police to ignore the Juvenile Justice Act. This is an enforcement crime.
* The station house officers simply refused to register FIRs and therefore the complainants had to approach higher ups, Government and courts to file complaints. Seeing the malpractice in police administration, the Code of Criminal Procedure—1973 gives special provisions to approach higher authorities in all cases if FI Rs are not registered by station house officers.
* Police may treat criminal cases as petitions, non-cognizable cases as cognizable by adding serious sections in the FIR, or vice-a-versa. If they do so, it is indeed extremely difficult to proceed further in the right direction. To get justice in such cases is highly expensive and time consuming.

The list of enforcement criminality may be endless. The purpose of resposible policing is administration of just justice and it may not be justifiable to invite higher authorities, Government, courts, media, politicians to intervene during various stages of police functionings. Policing a society has its sublimity and at any stage of policing, officers or policemen must not take law in their hands. The real purpose of policing is to ensure and, ordered social coexistence in true justice and in such a milieu, there is no scope for any sort of enforcement criminality. Precisely for this reason, every policeman/officer must guarantee that all members of the society have trust and confidence in the police way of administering justice. No society can tolerate enforcement crimes or can legitimize a wrong thing done by the enforcement machinery. Some police officers/men or for that matter, the entire police hierarchy may tolerate some enforcement crimes, but it can in no way claim to be based on respect for the justice or human conscience. Police has a duty to protect itself against abuses which may take place in the name of justice administration or under the pretext of administering justice.

Enforcement Crimes, Convictional Crimes, White Collar Crimes and no Collar Crimes

Enforcement crimes, more often than not, are not convictional crimes. Convictional crimes are those crimes in which the offender is convinced about committing the crimes. He has no option other than committing crimes. Terrorists, naxalites, political criminals are examples in point. In enforcement crimes, the offender commits crimes not because he is convinced about the need to commit crimes, but because he thinks that he can afford to do so without any evil consequences;

* A police officer keeps a detinue in nakedness as a precaution against suicide.
* A police officer requests for extending judicial remand even when he is convinced that the continued stay of the suspect is not necessary.

* A police officer handcuffs a suspect even when he does not think that he is of violent nature.

In all enforcement crimes one may see misuse of authority or abuse of power. The enforcement criminal commits crime under the colour of his official position and authority. A convictional offender may not have any official position or authority for misusing or abusing it. The enforcement criminal may advance arguments to convince people that he resorts to enforcement crimes because he is convinced about the need for them. He may argue that he is morally convinced although he has no legal justification for the act he does. He may further put forward more arguments to convince others that he does not have any personal interest in the matter; rather he does so because of the common good of the society. He fails to understand that the common good is best safeguarded when personal rights and individual freedoms are guaranteed. The law enforcement officer must ensure that people's rights are recognized, respected, co-ordinated, defended and promoted when he performs his manifold duties as a public servant. Any police officer who refuses to accept and recognize human rights or acts in violation of the Constitutional safeguards will not only fail in his duty but also his acts will be wholly lacking in force.

White collar crimes, as Prof. Edwin H. Sutherland says, are the crimes committed by people of high socio-economic status during the course of their profession. The intention here is mainly to make money and he considers the acts as violations of law. Enforcement crimes, of course, are committed during the course of one's performance of duty. But, invariably, he is a law enforcement officer. The victim of white collar crimes may not know that he is offended against by the white collar criminal. For, the victim yields to the desires of the offender. The victim may be benefitted by becoming so. In the case of enforcement criminality, the victim knows that he is offended against, but he suffers as he is helpless. He tolerates it as he knows that he cannot fight against a mammoth law enforcement agency.

White collar criminals are people of high socio-economic status whereas the policemen (constables) are not rated to be of such a high status as doctors, engineers, chartered accountants. Yet, the cop-whatever designation he has, can misuse his position to commit crimes.

* Constables travelling in a public conveyance omnibus without purchasing tickets or an officer who makes use of a taxi-cab without paying the taxi-fare, a superintendent of police who receives regular pay off from interest-groups and a director general of police who misuses his official vehicle for personal use—all of them are classified as enforcement offenders.

Both, white collar criminals and enforcement offenders, lack an upright conscience—that they do not have guilt feelings whenever they involve in the commission of crimes. Perhaps, the statutes in the country so far did not consider these offences as crimes under their provisions. On a closer scrutiny, it may be seen that everyone's conscience, rightly, accepts these crimes as violation of law. That may be the reason why departmental actions are initiated whenever offences of this nature are reported. This lenient approach mitigates the seriousness of the offence so much so that the enforcement offenders do not consider themselves as violators of law.

No collar crimes are traditional crimes and they include murder, rape, theft, burglary, etc. When a person commits such a crime, the law is set into motion. He is arrested, detained, remanded, prosecuted and tried. Law enforcement officers too can commit traditional crimes, but they are not seriously viewed. Use of third degree methods, calling of epithets, illegal detention (wrongful confinement), informal arrest (abduction), etc., are regarded as traditional crimes. But, when they are committed by law enforcement officers, then they are treated, if possible, as necessary evils for performing their duties for the common good of the society. This sort of double approach made the people and police personnel to consider such crimes as no crimes under the penal laws. Today, owing to the greater acceptance of human rights, such crimes, when committed by police, are dealt with as traditional crimes committed by law enforcement agencies. The case is then investigated by the police and this shows that some of the enforcement crimes become traditional crimes now.

Enforcement Crimes in Other Government Departments

No government department is exempted from the commission of enforcement crimes. Anybody who has a power to make decisions or who enjoys discretion in decision making may be able to commit enforcement crimes for lucrative or other purposes. He can think 'how a thing can not be done smoothly' and he can cause hurdles on the way. He can also think 'how a thing can be done'and in the latter case, it may be to the advantage, of the people. Corruption, bribery, graft, undue favours, etc, may be the advantages of involving oneself in enforcement crimes. Unlike the police, the enforcement crimes committed in other department are not very conspicuous. Though education, health, telephones, etc, are not strictly enforcement departments, yet a lot of enforcement crimes may take place in such departments. Recently, a paper reported that maximum number of human rights violations as revealed from the complaints received by the Human Rights Commission in a south Indian state—took place in schools and educational institutions which was followed by hospitals and health departments. Many government departments do not have any power or authority to interfere with the life or liberty of the people and as such people tolerate the harassment caused to them. But, the people raise their voice against the police, whenever enforcement crimes are committed as the police interfere with the life or liberty of the people. Many government departments do not take up any accountability for what they do and so long as there is no accountability for what they do, enforcement crimes will continue to be committed by them with immunity. The people will become the victims and sufferers of harassment.

There is no official or academic study available in India on the extent of enforcement crimes in police and other government departments. One reason for it is that the concept of 'enforcement crime' is of recent origin and the people have not looked at the activities of government departments from the point of view of enforcement criminality. Misguiding, furnishing false information, suppressing facts, suggesting falsehood, misdirecting, harassing, victimising, delaying decisions, hoarding of files, destroying files or papers kept in a file, burying files/ information, etc, may be considereu as enforcement crimes as they affect adversely the outcome in the matter.

Enforcement criminals are a privileged lot as they do not have any serious accountability over the crimes they commit. They are ensured of the salary and by committing enforcement crimes, they earn further income, advantages or favours. Take for example the case of an employee who was suspended from service for allegedly causing a vehicle accident. The government claimed that there was a loss of one lakh rupees as the vehicle involved in the accident belonged to the Government. The Government wanted to recover the amount from the suspended employee. To cut short, the inquiry, movement of files up and down, litigation on the issue in courts of law including the high court of the State, further inquiry by the vigilance and anti-corruption bureau, etc, took more than 5 lakhs rupees to the Government and Rs. 50,000 to the suspended employee. Who was benefitted by such enforcement crimes? In order to recover 1 lakh rupees, the Government send Rs. 5 lakhs and ultimately, the Government could not recover the amount, rather had a loss of Rs. 5 lakhs. Who is responsible for it? The public are not concerned about these colossal wastes of money caused to public exchequer by enforcement criminals. The people are concerned only with traditional crimes committed by ordinary people in society. They are ignorant about many of the enforcement crimes. Misuse of vehicles, telecommunication facilities, official stationary, etc, are nothing when the loss caused by wrong decisions is computed. People and their government suffer the enforcement crimes and criminals as they have no option other than doing so. One of the main reasons is that there are no penal statutes which treat enforcement crimes as punishable acts. Excepting corruption and bribery, all other enforcement crimes are just ignored by the people and the government.

Loss caused by Enforcement Criminals

The financial loss caused to the people and to the government by the enforcement criminals may be several times more than the loss caused by thieves, burglars, pick-pockets or similar traditional crime-doers. Delay in the encashment of bill for a contractor can cause heavy financial loss to him. Delay in conducting a surgery may cause the death of the patient. Delay in issuing certificates in time may cause rejection of the application for job/further studies. Delay in decision making may cause irrepairable damage to many. Thus, one may list out the ways and methods of committing various types of enforcement crimes and one may be surprised to see that the quantum of enforcement crimes committed by government departments may be beyond imagination.

Recently, a lawyer told me: "If FIRs are prepared for the enforcement crimes committed in various government departments, then more number of FIRs may have to be prepared in Government departments than the number of FIRs prepared for the various crimes committed by people in society". Though it was only a casual comment, there is a lot of truth in that. For, though enforcement criminals are only a few in number when compared to the population in the whole country, their crimes may outnumber the total number of traditional crimes committed by the entire population! Correspondingly, the financial loss caused by the enforcement criminals may be unimaginable. The financial loss caused by the thieves, burglars, pickpockets, and so on, in the entire country may be one thousand (or more) crores of rupees. But, the financial loss caused by the enforcement criminals is found to be several hundred crores and the people are blissfully ignorant about it. A single transaction may result in a financial loss of one thousand or several thousand crores of ruprees; "Everybody's business is nobody's business and Government business is everybody's business", and if this is true, the financial loss caused by enforcement criminals will be an amount which only imagination can conceive of. In the absence of any reliable empirical data and research studies on the issue under discussion, there is no need to elaborate further on the topic.

Police, Enforcement Crime and Loss

Everything is limited in time and space and administration of justice is not an exception to the general rule. When a crime is registered by police, there is no meaning in prolonging investigation beyond time and space. Everything must have a finality in time, but instances are plenty to show that investigation continues for several years or decades. The result is irrepairable damages to the suspects. In one instance, investigation continued for more than ten years and the suspects in the crime suffered under many counts. Psychological pain, social humiliation, traumatic experiences, financial loss, loss of employment, etc, are some among the many. Prolonged investigation of crime means miscarriage of justice and the law does not prescribe limitation to the investigation processes. Nobody seems to be accountable for the prolonged investigation and consequent losses which in financial terms may range from thousands to lakhs of rupees.

Crimes are investigated, prosecuted, tried and acquitted/convicted. In the case of acquittals, the entire exercise becomes futile and the accused becomes a victim of official actions done in the name of justice administration or in the pretext of administering justice. A police officer once told me: "cases will be ultimately acquitted. The harassment to the suspects, in police stations, lawyers offices, Verandah of the courts and the accused's boxes are the real punishment. They can be deterred from committing crimes by these pre-trial and trial procedures". What does it mean? It means that conviction is not the end of criminal investigations and prosecutions. The objective of criminal justice thus becomes harassment and victimisation of the suspects/accused in crime! Is it not an enforcement crime to do so? And who is accountable for the miscarriage of justice?

When criminal cases are acquitted, nobody bothers about the expenditure incurred by the State's exchequer for them. Acquittals reveal that there is a failure in the principles contained in 'management by objectives'. As it is today, more criminal cases are acquitted in India and the loss caused to the exchequer is borne by the people. As the amount is diffused among the general public, no one has any direct loss or sufferings. But, it affects the trust and confidence of the people on the various sub-systems that operate for administration of justice. When more and more cases are acquitted, people start thinking about the futility of the enforcement procedures and criminal justice administration.

What is the loss suffered by the acquitted in criminal cases.? No one has any accurate account of the same, yet it runs into several thousands. People have broken or become paupers by the time acquittal verdicts are pronounced. If acquittal verdicts come out as a result of perfunctory investigation or indifferent prosecution, then, who must bear the loss caused to the exchequer and to the accused? At present, there is no law to realize the lost amount from people who are responsible for such enforcement crimes. There is a school of thought which advocates that the people and the accused cannot afford to suffer loss in such instances and precisely therefore the individuals responsible for causing miscarriage of justice must bear the loss caused by them to the State and to the accused.

Instances have been reported that the police have registered false cases or chargesheeted people on civil matters, etc. No doubt, they are enforcement crimes and human rights activists argue that the victims of the abuse of power and authority have legitimate claim for getting damages for the loss sustained by them in such cases.

Victimology is a developed branch of science in criminology.

Equal Justice System which is now being accepted thinks that the law enforcement and justice administration have accountability to (1) the crime-doers, (2) to the victims of crime/abuse of power and authority, (3) to the society, and (4) to the justice system itself. Such a system cannot tolerate enforcement crimes. The system enumerates enforcement crimes under several heads and they are:

1. ***Enforcement crimes during law and order:*** They include patrolling in an indifferent, beat in a ritualistic manner, use of excessive force during a *lathy* charge, provocative behaviour at a scene of law and order, partisan attitude in a communal violence, insensitive behaviour during student violence, indiscriminate firing at angry mobs, unjustifiable arrests and preventive detentions and many such activities.

2. ***Enforcement crimes during prevention of crimes:*** Include lethargic actions, indifferent strategies taking of no preventive steps, no caution approach, failure to stop conducive atmosphere in crime prone areas, neglect of keeping surveillance of bad characters, omitting to initiate preventive patrolling, shadowing of suspects, keeping watch of hardened criminals and failure to collect proper intelligence, etc.

3. ***Enforcement crimes during investigation of crime:*** Include informal arrest, illegal detention, humiliating treatment in lock ups, coercion and use of third degree methods during interrogation, callous and culpable attitude towards witnesses, production of tutored witnesses, manipulation of records, concoction of evidence, registering of false cases, perfunctory investigation, neglect of inspection of the scene of crime, etc.

4. ***Enforcement crimes during V.I.P. security duties:*** Include shouting at people and calling of epithets, causing of unnecessary road-blocks, unwanted body searches and undesirable ways of body searches, irritating behaviour and illegal arrests, undesirable questionings of people and objectionable manners etc.

5. ***Enforcement crimes during traffic control include:*** Shouting at drivers, unnecessary detention of vehicles on roads, undesirable ways of behaviour and manners, use of obscene words to road users and vehicle drivers and autorikshaw/taxi drivers, vehicles checks at odd hours, corruption and bribery, etc.

6. ***Enforcement crimes during collection of intelligence include:*** Haphazard ways of intelligence collection, indifferent assessment and evaluation, wrong interpretations and follow up actions, dissemination of false information and speculated ideas, armchair collection of intelligence, telephonic frauds, imaginative interpretations, spicy reportings, hollow observations, reporting to please authorities, etc.

7. ***Enforcement crimes in disciplinary proceedings:*** Include initiation of disciplinary actions out of hostility, enemity, vengeance and vindictiveness, unnecessary suspensions, refusal or failure to review suspensions, purposeful delay to give subsistence allowance and to reinstatement, prolonged inquiries, inquiries with bias and in violation of the principles of natural justice, unjustifiable awarding of punishments, etc.

8. ***Enforcement crimes during natural calamities:*** Include thieving articles, ornaments and property, misbehaviour with people, misappropriation or fraud, propagation of false news, discriminate treatments to the victims of natural calamities, plundering of wealth, ill treatment to women and girls, neglect of the old and infirm, insensitive treatment to the depressed, etc.

9. ***Enforcement crimes during human rights enforcement:*** Include behaviour showing, lack of respect to human dignity, violations of the principles of gender justice, juvenile justice, etc., unnecessary handcuffing, keeping the suspects in nakedness/half nakedness in police lock ups, unscientific ways

of questioning, etc.

10. ***Enforcement crimes during police administration:*** Include vindictive annual confidential report writing, preferred treatment to subordinates, neglect of duties, favouritism, partiality and parochialism, communalism, political affiliations, hostility, inter-personnel rivalry, unethical ways of behaviour, harassment and victimization, etc.

Enforcement crimes may be visible or invisible and so long as there does not exist enough transparency, it is likely that same crimes go unnoticed by many in the department.

Enforcement Crimes and Compensation to the Victims

People all over the world have started to recognize more and more enforcement crimes although they have not given any special or specific identity for such crimes in statutory penal laws.

* Bureaucratic hoarding of files for the purpose of laying decisions must be treated as a crime for the purpose of claiming compensation. The argument in this direction is receiving good acceptance from the public. Today, some people approach courts of law to get compensation for the loss sustained by them as a result of delayed decisions from the bureaucracy. As the court proceedings may be expensive, some are not inclined to go to courts of law to claim damages and therefore the argument is that provision must be made in the law in such a way that the enforcement criminal who hoards files for delaying decisions must be punished and must be made liable to compensate the victim/s of his abuse of power and authority.

* After a *lathy* charge or firing, politicians and people make a hue and cry to conduct inquiries and sometimes insist on judicial probes. They want the guilty officers to be placed under suspension and the Government may be forced to answer a number of questions in the Legislature/Parliament. If judicial probes or executive inquiries prove that excessive force is employed, then

departmental actions and even criminal cases are initiated. People may also rush to courts of law for getting damages. In a particular police operation in a South Indian State, there arose a number of allegations against police officers for gender indecent behaviour to women/girls and they had to answer a number of suits filed before the courts of law. Public interest litigations too are filed in some instances. The courts allow compensation of the victims of police inaction, overaction and illegal actions. It shows that there is an increasing acceptance of victimological contents in enforcement crimes.

* Whenever the police are lethargic or show indifferent attitude to prevention of crimes, the press and the people react to them. Letters to the editors are written and the attention of police authorities are called to initiate steps. Instances are plenty that the press write editorials on police inaction. Discussions are held in electronic media and features and serialized articles are brought out in periodicals. In some cases, *suo moto* actions are initiated by courts. The net result is that the press, people, court and the media pressure the police to be vigilant and thus to avoid enforcement criminality.

* Human Rights Commission are approached by the people for human rights violations by police. In some States, human rights courts are functioning. In a South Indian State, massive Statewide campaign was organized to create awareness of human rights among police personnel working at the cutting edge level. A number of inservice courses on human rights have been organized in the State Police Training College. The impact has been that human rights violations by police have been considerably reduced owing to the special awareness campaigns and specialized courses. Recently, the Chairperson of the State Human Rights Commission made a public utterance revealing that complaints on human rights violations by police in that State have come out considerably. It shows that enforcement

crimes violating the human rights of people are lowering down in the society.

* Conscious attempts are made to inculcate scientific knowledge in interrogation of suspects. A lot of scientific methods are initiated in many areas of police investigation. Computerized finger printing, computer searches, forensic exmination of physical evidence, modernization of modus operandi bureau, etc, are undertaken on a war-footing. This has come into being as a result of public reactions towards antiquated methods of crime investigation and employment of unscientific techniques during investigation of crimes. People are showing their uneasiness, intolerance, antipathy and aggressiveness towards enforcement crimes. Strictures are passed by courts of law whenever they see concocted evidence or production of tutored witnesses. Many voluntary agencies are coming forward to offer free legal aid to the accused in crimes. Human rights activists keep a vigil on police against enforcement crimes and in a nutshell, the police are handcuffed in many ways. Nevertheless, there is allegation that the police hierarchy has not become sensitive to public demands even now. They fail to recognize enforcement crimes and resultantly some in police service continue to be committing enforcement crimes in various ways.

* During VIP's visits, the police take extra care to see that they give protection to the VIP. complaints regarding indecent behaviour towards the people during a VIP's visit are coming down. Road blocks are enforced with caution causing least inconvenience to the public. People are telling that the road-blocks created by the administration just to provide safety for the VIP is a human right violation. The approach and outlook of the authorities towards road blocks is undergoing a change.

* Disciplinary proceedings and enforcement crimes by authorities become a topic of discussion howadays. There is the de-

mand to establish special Disciplinary Tribunals in police department. As the police department has many disciplinary proceedings, the members of the service demand just justice during disciplinary proceedings. In a South Indian State, regular courses on disciplinary proceedings are organized to educate the inquiring authority to conduct the inquiries in a quasi-judicial way—keeping the principles of natural justice. Studies conducted on disciplinary inquiries in police show that some of them are initiated out of hostility, vindictiveness and with an intention to cause calculated harassment to subordinate ranks.

In a western country, the law is that the delinquent under inquiry must be compensated for the loss he sustained owing to disciplinary action in all cases he has been exonerated from the charges levelled against him. The western law says further that disciplinary action should be initiated against the disciplinary authority for initiating departmental actions in a malefide manner or with vindictiveness. In India, such laws are not in existence. Nevertheless the move is to enact such laws ensuring victimological compensation to the victimzed employee in case injustice has been done to him. Enforcement crimes committed hierarchy by misusing their power cannot be tolerated.

* People make representations to higher authorities or approach Administrative Tribunals/High Courts with grievances whenever they see that administrative injustice has been done to them. The lower level functionaries do not do so because of the expenses involved in such legal battles. But, today, there is a trend to move the courts to get administrative justice even by lower level functionaries in police.

India is a democracy and the ruler cannot commit enforcement crimes. 'The king commits no crime' is not accepted, so much so, that all want enforcement justice wherever possible.

In spite of the changes in outlook and increased crimes, there take place a number of enforcement crimes in police. Anything that has a beginning in the past—that has developed over a period of time—that has established a pattern of behaviour—can not be easily wiped off overnight. It requires time and it is hoped, the police is moving towards a brighter tomorrow where thre will be more transparency and more accountablity to people, the patrons in a democracy.

The movement towards handcuffing the police from committing enforcement crimes may be painful for a group of police officers who still have wrong impressions about responsible policing in a democracy. They do not think law enforcement from the citizens' point of view—from their patrons' point of view. The police have to think in a broader perspective—the perspective being that they are meant to protect certain important values in a liberal democracy. Any reason glorifying enforcement crimes, however forcefully presented, can never justify any sort of enforcement crimes in people's courts of justice.

References

1. Rochin V. California, 1952, 342 U.S. 165, 72 S.Ct. 205, 96 L. Ed. 183.
2. R.K. Pande V.State of Madhya Pradesh, A.I.R. 1975 S.C. 1026, 1975 Cr. L.J. 870.
3. Nandini Satpathy Vs. P.L. Dani, A.I.R. 1978 S.C. 1025.
4. Baladin V.State of Uttar Pradesh, A.I.R. 1956 S.C. 181.
5. Pandurang V.State of Hyderabad, A.I.R. 1955 S.C. 216; 1955 Cr. L.J. 572.

2
ORIGIN, DEVELOPMENT AND PERSISTENCE

The British brought the organized police system in India and they enacted the Indian Police Act on 1861. They had specific objectives for maintaining a police Force in India and their objectives were obvious. Enforcement crimes were unknown to them or if at all they knew them they never wanted the police to be enforcement crime-free in India. For enforcement crimes were necessary for their police to retain the British Raj in India. It is more than 50 years now since the people's police have come into being in India. The British police did establish a tradition of police behaviour and culture of police in which enforcement crimes were accepted. Nobody questioned the tradition and culture till India became independent. Or, if at all somebody wanted to question the tradition and culture, then he/she was not courageous enough to do so. For, in that case he/she would have been made a victim of police misbehaviour/abuse of power and authority. Victimological concepts were unheard then and victim justice was not known to any one then.

I met a British police officer a few days ago when I participated in a seminar organised by the British Library, Thiruvananthapuram. We had a long discussion and he emphatically told me: "If you do not like the British tradition and culture, you change them". Yes, there was a point in what he said. For, fifty long years have now elapsed since the British left India and they do not interfere in the police administration in India now.

He said further : "you, people could not enact a new Police Act for the democratic India. Do not break the mirror if you do not like your face". I thought then that there was a further point in what he said loudly. He continued: "Ever since I landed in India I hear many people—especially police officers blaming the British for the sad state of affairs in police administration. Blaming others is not a solution to any problem. Resolve the problem constructively".

I did not have counter arguments to attack him. For, I too am not interested to blame the British for what the police do today and now.

Enforcement crimes in police did not come up one day, too soon. Certainly, they had an origin and development. And the British was responsible once upon a time and there is no meaning or need to accuse them of what the police do *hic et hunc*.

"I am occupying the chair which was once occupied by an I.P. officer"—said a senior police officer to me.

"What did he mean by that"? I asked the question to myself and attempted to answer it. I understood that he had heard/read a lot about how the I.P. officers enjoyed their lives in Indian police. He wanted to enjoy his position as the I.P. officers enjoyed. In other words, he wanted to live among people as if I.P. officers lived fifty years ago. He never wanted to divorce himself from the decade old—past—police customs traditions and culture. If he thought so, then enforcement crimes had/have a place in police department yesterday and even today. So long as the Indian Police Act—1861, Indian Penal Code—1860, Code of Criminal Code-1973, Indian Evidence Act-1872 are in operation, enforcement crimes will be on the increase. Antiquated Acts, long tradition/culture centered police officers/men and most recent concepts like victim justice, equal justice, juvenile justice, enforcement justice, just justice, victim justice, etc, are mixed today so much so that enforcement crimes too become a part of police sub-culture. Nevertheless, people question the police when they see enforcement crimes.

Enforcement Crimes and Existing Laws

Indian Evidence Act says that nothing is admissible in evidence if it is told to a police officer or in his presence.

Accusatorial system of justice which is in vogue in India says that the accused is presumed to be innocent until he is proved to be guilty.

Police and prosecution must prove everything beyond any shadow of doubt. When two views are possible, the view favourable to the accused will be taken.

No force, false promises, coercion, undue influence, third degree methods should be used to elicit information from the suspect under interrogation.

A legal practitioner must be allowed to be present during interrogation—though not throughout the interrogation. "In the existing situation, how can the police perform their duties without committing enforcement crimes?"—asked a deputy inspector general of police in charge of crime investigation in a State. He means that it is virtually impossible to prove a crime without having recourse to some form of enforcement crimes. "We are not gods or demi-gods. We are human beings with limitations, weaknesses and frailties.

We can not be super-human"- He argued furiously. His argument shows that he is in a dilemma.

Yes, I could understand his problem. Hence I argued back: "O.K., you may have recourse to all sorts of enforcement crimes—namely, concoction of evidence, use of third degree, production of false witnesses and what not and then tell me, what are you going to achieve?" He told me: "Then, he may be punished" I asked: "Do you think that such a punishment is administration of justice—just justice?" I asked him: "If you employ the same method on an innocent man, then he too can be punished. Is it administration of justice—just justice?" I asked him further: "Do you think that the end justifies the means in justice administration? or If you are the suspect in a crime, will you advocate the strategies you are advocating now?". And the questions remain unanswered even today. Perhaps, professional training, acquisition of expertise, acquiring of knowledge and information and acceptance of the principles of human rights, code of conducts, Constitutional safeguards and international consensus reached on the issue may answer the questions in a meaningful manner. The principle followed everywhere is that the police must obey the law while enforcing the law. These laws are available in many countries and how do the police perform their duties in such countries.? Do they involve in committing enforcement crimes? What is the extent and intensity of custodial torture, custody-deaths, concoction of evidence by police etc.? Historians on police origin and development endorse the view that enforcement torture was the practice even before Torture Commission—1855. Laws were enacted to stop the malady, but in practical reality it continued to be in force. Even after independence, torture and enforcement crimes continued to be practiced. People raised their voice against the malpractices. Laws were further changed. Departmental instructions were issued. People reacted and now a situation has emerged and the people demand transparency, accountability and victimological compensation for enforcement crimes.

Symptoms of Human Behaviour and Enforcement Crimes

Crime is a human act being very much a social fact it is an accepted principle and therefore, it may be stated that enforcement crime in police is a police act and very much a social fact. If that is so, what to do?

There are a number of psychological theories and psychiatric approaches explaining the dynamics of human behaviour and especially criminal behaviour. The same theories and explanations are applicable in the case of enforcement crimes as well. The theories are not discussed in detail in this book. Nevertheless, how do the police show symptoms of enforcement crimes. The symptoms may be—in short—.

1. Enforcement criminals are found to be people suffering from feelings of inadequacy.
2. They have decreased effectiveness in job performance or suffer from decreased productivity at work.
3. They show symptoms of social withdrawal.
4. They may exhibit guilt over their past activities after the commission of enforcement crimes.
5. They have pessimism towards their future.

It is not necessary that they manifest all these symptoms. They may show some of them in a projected way. My studies on enforcement crime prone police officers men reveal that some of them have:

1. Inflated self esteem;
2. Hypersensitivity;
3. Excessive involvement in sadistic activities;
4. Physical restlessness;
5. Inappropriate laughing, joking, funning, etc.

In some police officers/ men, I could notice:

(i) Loss of self esteem;
(ii) Self depreciation;
(iii) Irritability;
(iv) Excessive anger/ hot-temperedness.

I have further noticed in some that they show -

(i) Pervasive and unwanted suspicion and mistrust of people. Any amount of evidence to rebut the suspicion does not work with them;

(ii) Restricted affectivity to people. They,want to show that they are dispassionate, objective and reasonable in their decisions and activities;

(iii) Hypervigilant and unsentimental approaches. They lack tender feelings;

(iv) Searching mentality for hidden motives and special meanings in others' behaviour;

(v) Argumentative character. They exaggerate and over—exaggerate things;

(vi) Tense always and are stubborn in approaches;

(vii) Self defence and non-acceptance criticisms against them;

(viii) Emotional coldness;

(ix) Lack of warmth and tender feelings towards others; and

(x) Agressiveness and hostility.

The officers/men who are enforcement crime-prone day dream a lot. They do not have confidence in many. Some may be good in self-dramatization which is shown by exaggerated expression of emotions. They may be ego-centric and interested in self-indulgence. They show over-reaction to minor events and become easily irritated at things which do not usually irritate ordinary people. They may be demanding a lot of things from others. They may exhibit irrational and angry outbursts or tantrums. They expect special favours from people and do not have any reciprocal desires.

I have observed in some senior police officers who showed enforcement crime-prone behaviour that they had grandiose sense of self- importance. They thought that they had a sort of uniqueness. I know an officer who used to be highly enforcement crime-prone in administration always telling about his uniqueness by exaggeration of his achievements and talents. He used to take advantage of others for self-aggrandizement.

Enforcement crime-prone officers/men are found to be preoccupied with fantacies of unlimited success, power, brilliance, etc. They are people who desire for constant and continuous attention and admiration. They do not show any regard for the rights of others and human rights. They express cool indifference and lack empathy.

People differ in their psychological characteristics when they exhibit enforcement crime-prone behaviours. Some may be crime-prone in investigation of crime while others may be so in law and order matters. Still others may be so in disciplinary actions or administration as the case may be.

Departmental Structure and Enforcement Crimes

Police department is hierarchical in structure and there exists the "parade ground discipline" in varying degrees in different police offices. Resultantly, the higher levels command and lower levels obey and it was more so in the past than what it is at present. Owing to the working of police associations and inculcation of democratic ideals, the police structure is now shaken to some extent. New channels of communication are coming up and there exists visible or invisible interference by vested interests resulting in enforcement crimes.

Imitation works as a force among the members of the service. They imitate others who exhibit enforcement crimes. Suggestion is another mechanism which works strongly. Enforcement crimes committed by one member have suggestive effects on people who have like-minded aptitudes. Identification is yet another mechanism. A director general of police used to threaten his subordinates telling that he might initiate disciplinary action against them. Subordinates used to tremble at the sight of the director general of police. Officers who have a similar mental make up thus started identifying with the director general of police and they liberally committed enforcement crimes to keep their subordinates within a circumscribing limit.

Association with fellow colleagues, superiors and subordinates make some to resort to enforcement criminality. They learn the methods of committing crimes and various ways and means to commit further crimes. Affinities with enforcement criminals give courage to some to commit crimes.

Police ecology is another cause of enforcement crimes. Every police officer lives in a 'functional rank' as sub-inspector, inspector, superintendent of police, inspector general of police, and so on. Naturally, the behaviour of the fellow colleagues and superiors in the hierarchy influences each one of them. In fact, for all practical purposes, one's interactions are limited to the people belonging to his functional area. By imitation, suggestion, identification, association, interactions, learning, etc, each one of them internalizes many things including enforcement criminality. This is called milieu influence in police ecology.

From my study, it is made clear to me that the effective milieu for the officers of the Indian police service is confined to their interactions among themselves and the same is applicable to officers belonging to the state police service, to the officers of the general executive, to the armed reserve or to the armed batallions. The constabulary forms another milieu and generally a constable is not very much influenced by the deputy inspector general of police who belongs to another functional milieu. The enforcement crimes committed by an inspector general of police may not be learnt by a sub-inspector who does not get opportunities to commit such crimes.

Opportunity theory also explains the why of enforcement crimes. The more the opportunities are provided for a person to involve himself to commit enforcement crime, the more likely it is the he becomes an enforcement criminal. Prof. Edwin H. Sutherland says :"Criminal behaviour is learnt. It is learnt in interaction with other persons in a process of communication. The communication can be often verbal and at times through gestures".

"The principal part of the learning, Prof. Sutherland continues,"of criminal behaviour occurs within intimate personal groups. And, when criminal behaviour is learnt, the learning includes: (1) techniques of committing crimes (2) the specific directions of motives, drives, rationalization and attitudes. The specific direction of motives and drives is learnt from definition of legal codes as favourable or unfavourable[1]".

Moral Consciousness and Enforcement Crimes

Enforcement crimes are moral evils and doubtlessly, the moral consciousness has a decisive role to play in the commission of enforcement crimes. In my book *Indian police—2001 : What Went Wrong Here* ? I have discussed some aspects of police morality. mentioning that police morality was something nobody took seriously.

There is a view - i.e., 'Police Conscience' is something different from 'Human Consience'. In other words, what may be immoral in 'Human Conscience' can be thought of as quite moral in police conscience. I, for one, cannot understand it. A policeman is first of all a man and then only he becomes a policeman. He possesses a human conscience and not a police conscience . If every profession has a conscience different in nature, then the concept of human conscience may become unclear.

"Do good and avoid evil"—this is a general law of morality and it is so in police life. Moral wrecks are seen in all professions and police is not an exception. Police officers/men who commit enforcement crimes may be "moral wrecks". Police behaviour has to be guided by objective norms and these objective norms are written in the conscience of every policeman/officer. If he does not abide by such norms, then he is a moral wreck. If he thinks that custodial rape is a desirable thing or victimization of his subordinates is a good thing, it means that he lacks moral conscience.

Human conscience and police conscience—are they two consciences ? Human conscience is something that is seen in the human mind. It is developed by the conscience formation agencies. "Never victimize a subordinate out of vindictiveness or personal hostility"—this is a moral principle which is in the human conscience. But, in a given situation, one decides to victimize a subordinate and in so doing, he employs his subjective scales of morality. He finds justification for what he does and in so doing he is committing an enforcement crime. Moralists may argue that it is the human conscience that must guide the human activities.

Police conscience which finds justification in doing things such as concoction of evidence in a criminal case, registration of false cases thus encourages immoral activities which the human conscience does not accept. My researches show that the subjectively formed police conscience works as a powerful etiological factor in committing enforcement crimes in police work.

Police conscience is formed and developed only after one has enlisted himself or herself as a police officer/man (woman). A new recruit to the police department is taught that torture of property offenders in police custody to elicit a confession is justified for the common good of the society. As he is in the age group of 20-30 years when this morality is inculcated to him in police service, he understands that it is a forbidden act, but a desirable one. Yet, he thinks that torturing a man is a moral wrong - a legally forbidden act—a socially unacceptable behaviour. He become confused. He evaluates the pros and cons of torturing a property offender in police custody and then takes a decision to torture or not to torture a person in police custody. A mature police officer is one who is able to take evaluative decisions. He must be sensitive to human values, human rights values, Constitutional and other legal values when he evaluates an issue. In police training institutions, there is no attempt made to inculcate moral values to the trainees. Trainers must inculcate in their trainees an evaluative/appreciative moral knowledge. At present, there are many police officers/men who had no source to obtain correct moral knowledge in police work. Ethics is not taught. Code of conduct is not clearly told to them. The intellectual training confines mostly to the study of penal, procedural and evidence laws. There is a view that every police trainee must be given guided opportunities to discuss, debate and role-play about police morality by clarifying the norms and values involved in police work and thereby provide opportunities for the development of a morality based police personality. If the police department wants to have an enforcement crime-free administration, then the young recruits and raw trainees must be encouraged to take interest in moral learning and the department must help them to reflect over their doings on the basis of the norms and values involved.

Autonomy, Integration, Prudence, Sincerity and Enforcement Crimes

A police officer does not detain a suspect beyond 24 hours—why ? He does not do so because he is afraid of the legal complications and punishment if he does so. His action is based on the fear of punishment. He is not doing so out of his personal conviction —a moral sense—out of his respect for law as a law enforcement officer. Hence, it may be argued that enforcement crime can be reduced if one behaves out of his personal convictions. Reduction of enforcement crimes must proceed from his inner and autonomous conscience. The police officer who behaves from his self conviction, inner motive and autonomous conscience sees himself as a member of the responsible police service and contributes to the common good and just justice administration. For him the moral principles become self—accepted principles. He respects the dignity, freedom and rights of the human person. Police conscience accepts the principles of law and morality. Every police officer/man must be inspired and persuaded to abide by the principles accepted by the international community from the moment he enters into police service.

In police training institutions, the trainees are taken to the parade ground and are taught a parade ground morality. If the disciplinary techniques usually employed by the physical training instructors are rather punishments, then it is likely to create in the newly entered trainees deep-rooted fear and the result is that he expresses a sort of parade ground discipline in his interpersonnel relationship with superiors. At the same time, in his relationship with subordinates and people outside, he may exhibit an authoritarian personality. A trainee must be corrected with understanding when mistakes are committed. He should be given, under proper guidance, sufficient space and scope for developing a healthy autonomy.

A police officer who catches hold of a person for causing grievious hurt to another must not hurt the crime-doer. If he does so, he goes against his own judgement and conviction. If he employs torture on the suspect, then it must cause a certain amount of guilt in him. An upright conscience is the ability for integrated and positive value based behaviour. Police functionaries must have a mature integrated conscience if they want to reduce the number of enforcement crimes. An integrated conscience requires good moral training.

Prudence is a quality. In order to become prudent in actions, police officers/men need knowledge, life experience, insight into the issue and a sense of realism. Police training must aim at developing prudence in officers/men so that they will have a mature conscience which alone can reduce enforcement criminality. They must be sincere in thinking, words and actions. At a given situation, police conscience, self conscience and human conscience may work. There will be a harmony among them if the officer/man is sincere and honest.

Sub-Culture and Enforcement Crimes

In 1978, a deputy inspector general of police told me : "Police is the coercive weapon of the Government".

I asked him : "Which or whose Government ?".

He said : " Of the Government in power or the ruling Government".

I said : "In a democracy, governments come and go. And if the police is going to be the coercive weapon of the Government in power, then the police may fail to fulfill its mission in a democracy".

I could learn from his face that he was feeling uneasy to listen to my argument. Yes, Indian police was the coercive weapon of the British Government and there was only one Government in power and that was the "Government in London". Whatever that be, the police officer/man who was a government servant—submissive and docile—during the British regime continued to be so even after India became independent in 1947. Police officer/man became a 'public servant' after India's independence, nevertheless, very senior police officers, even in 1978 thought that they were only government servants and were the coercive weapon of the ruling government in power. In a democracy, the opposition is as powerful as the ruling political parties. As the wrong idea was taught to police (i.e. police is the coercive weapon of the government in power) trainees for decades even after India's independence, the police in India became the spatula of the political parties in power. This resulted in the commission of a variety of enforcement crimes for pleasing politicians and political parties. National Police Commission in its report has emphasised the need to take away/minimize political interference in police work. The culture or sub-culture prevailing in police today is "spatular submissiveness" to political parties in power. This certainly is a powerful cause of enforcement crimes.

Till recently and even today, police trainees are taught that they are a part of the coercive rule of the government in power. Political parties have their vested interests which the police does not have. The police has to work under the Constitution of India and the laws made thereunder. There is a feeling that there exists a value conflict between the political culture (values) and police sub-culture (values). In certain occasions, political parties may make attempts to misuse the police powers/authority for political advantage. Thus, the police becomes a weapon in their hands for getting political mileage for them. The police officers and men are yet to be taught that police values are different from political values.

The "coercive weapon" theory that has gone deep into police

sub-culture made the police to think that they could use force on anybody at any time. In the past, the police, worked as a terrorizing force and the people used to tremble at the sight of a policeman. They committed a lot of enforcement crimes then and there was nobody to question them. Parents, grandparents, and so on, used to threaten or frighten their children/grandchildren by telling that the police would be called in case they disobeyed them. So much was the fear of the "coercive weapon" caused among the people that people used to look at police sub-culture as a culture of torture and coerciveness. However, owing to the development of human rights consciousness among the people and the police, the "coercive or torture" culture of police is getting changed. Consequently, enforcement crimes too come down in police sub-culture.

People see how the police behave in other democracies in the world through electronic and print media and they expect the police in India to behave the way the police in other parts of the world behave. There exists a conflict between people's expectations and police behaviour. The people's expectations and police obligations do not coincide and the result is lack of appreciation for what the police do for the people. Enforcement crimes can be put down only if the police make conscious attempts to behave the way people expect them to behave.

The various ways police involve themselves in the commission of many types of enforcement crimes, which would be interpreted by them as necessary evils done for the service of the people in a democracy, actually open the new doors to new threats against human welfare and common good. Apart from the fact that these enforcement crimes are socially, culturally and morally unacceptable to people in society since they keep away the people from police, these enforcement crimes have high degree of failure, not just a failure to maintain good police-citizen relations but with regard to the administration of just justice in society. Among the people, the sense of anguish, of severe discomfort and even of desperation gets multiplied when they see the police involving themselves in the commission of enforcement crimes. Such a serious situation can and does threaten the already fragile equilibrium of people's life in a democratic set up.

Lack of Self Esteem and Enforcement Crimes

On the one hand people, law and the police say that the value and dignity of every individual as a human being must be acknowledged and respected. There must not be any distinction of caste, status, political affiliations and economic positions. On the other hand, this desire is contradicted by a tragic repudiation of it in police sub-culture. This denial is found to be the distressing and indeed more scandalous effect of a lack of self esteem among police functionaries. A police officer/ man who has a self-esteem can not and does not commit enforcement crimes as enforcement crimes are threats to the entire culture of justice and human rights. Enforcement crimes jeoparadize the very meaning of policing a society. Police in such situations aggravate situations of injustice in which the life of the entire people is degraded and trampled upon.

Misconceived and Perverted Ego Concepts and Enforcement Crimes

What are the ego concepts of police officers? In the existing legal system, the police have a lot of powers—of course, with limitations. They can misuse them if they want. Instances are plenty to show that some do misuse their power and authority. Some do so because of their misconceived and perverted ego-concepts.

"I can see that you are put behind the bars"—said a police officer once to a person who refused to obey an illegal order given in a petition inquiry.

"Don't play with me. I am a police officer"—angrily said another police officer. Yes, he was a police officer and he could do only those things empowered by law and nothing more. But, his words signified that he might resort to enforcement crimes if he so wanted.

No doubt, the criminal laws in the country are so many and so comprehensive that any human act can be interpreted as violation of law with some justifications if a police officer so desires. If no legal provision is found, then he can find out some section of law and register a case against anyone. In one case, a police officer was alleged to have put *ganja* in a vehicle belonging to someone whom he did not like. Later a case was registered under NDPS Act. In disciplinary proceedings, one may see many cases of superiors expressing their perverted ego-concepts and pasted glories.

Officers/men who have misconceived ideas about their ego are people who are unable to accept their authority as the "supreme gift" of the people for whose welfare and protection they are appointed in service. They are expected to show responsible responsibility in their activities.

Certainly, there exists a clash between the good and bad within a person. Every police officer is not only faced with but necessarily in the midst of this conflict. In every such situation, one must have an inescapable responsibility of choosing to be unconditionally pro-justice. This, if one can have, is what is called the correct perception of one's ego as a police officer/man committed to the cause of justice.

An assistant superintendent of police who was posted in a police station to do his practical training once told his sub-inspector/constables that he would see them "well", when he was given full and independent charge in a sub-division training. He wanted a car to take his family to a tourist spot for enjoyment and car should be arranged at the sub-inspector's expense. He wanted a female cook for his kitchen and he expected it to be done by his constables. He wanted a table lamp and he wanted it to be purchased by his assistant sub-inspector. His demands were many and he thought that he could get all of them materialized through others who worked under him. No doubt, he was a person with perverted values and wrong ego-concepts. Such people do a lot of damage to the reputation of the department. No rank, no position, no status, no education, no ego-concepts, no circumstances, no purpose, no authority, no power whatsoever can ever make licit an enforcement crime which is intrinsically illicit. The subordinates condemn such behaviours which are calculated to exploit and plunder the subordinates helpless 'submissiveness' to higher authorities.

Sub-Sub Culture in Police and Enforcement Crimes

Police constables have a sub-culture within the sub-culture of police. The sub-inspectors have a sub-culture within the police sub-culture. Officers of the Indian police service have a sub-culture within the sub-culture of police. Or better, every rank in police has a sub-culture of its own and the enforcement crimes are specific and peculiar to each sub-culture. The constables' sub-culture commits enforcement crimes within their sub-culture and mostly they will be against the people in society. They may use filthy language or call epithets. They may receive bribery or may show an indifferent attitude to crimes in society. The sub-inspectors may commit crimes against their subordinates and against the general public. He may make use of the constables as collection-agents of corruption money or harass constables for not listening to his unlawful orders. A superintendent of police has wider powers and precisely therefore he has wider scope for committing more enforcement crimes against many subordinates and the people in society. A superintendent of police in the Indian police service purchased two cars, one residential flat and a plot besides a palatial house he constructed during a period of 5 years in his service. He came from a moderately rich family and he became rich all of a sudden and some other officers of the Indian police service could not become that affluent even after 15 years of service. Wife, wife's fortune, wife's income, etc, were explanations for his affluence, but they could not convince many working with him. For, many of them knew how he made money and certainly, enforcement crimes were a fertile source of income for him. Whatever that be, he found difficulty to convince himself that he made his fortune through licit means.

Enforcement Crimes and Police Hierarchy

Enforcement crimes committed by many are usually taken note of by colleagues, associates, superiors and subordinates. As many are indulged in some form or other of enforcement crimes, some tolerate them, others show an indifferent attitude and yet others express positive encouragement, etc. Many police officers think that tolerance, indifference and encouragement, etc, are necessary for departmental coexistence. At the basis of all these tolerance, indifference and encouragement lies the ethical relativism which alone guarantees to them the mutual respect.

Once a superintendent of police (as he then was) in the Indian police service went to the director general of police and became very close. He made him believe that he would write three books in his name so that the name of the director general of police would be indelibly written in golden letters in the history of police in that State. Believing everything the 'learned' superintendent said, the director general of police made a press release stating that he would author three books soon. To cut short, the director general of police retired on superannuation and the superintendent of police did nothing towards the achievement of his promise to the director general of police. The superintendent was there to exploit his "closeness" with the director general for his personal advantage. It is learnt that he could cash in on his contacts to the disadvantage of many who worked with him. The superintendent of police was evaluated as a man of low values and his ways of behaviour were afterwards known as Alexism which I have defined in my book titled *Management Thoughts on Police Administration*[2]. Alexism, as it is known now, too is an enforcement crime against God and man. 'Alexism', I consider, is an enforcement crime which no law—moral, social, cultural, religious, personal — can claim to legitimize.

Departmental Shortcomings and Enforcement Crimes

As indicated earlier, enforcement crimes in police department had originated long back and have developed over many decades—

and still continue to persist in police sub-culture. I asked some of the lower level officer trainees to frankly tell me the why of such persistence. They advanced many reasons and some of them are:

1. Disparity in pay between the constable at the bottom and the director general at the top;

2. Lack of promotion prospects for the lowest levels of police administration

3. Lack of self-esteem of the departmental higher ups and their willful negligence to remedy the departmental shortcomings. Example, the higher—highest high and the high est have every human comforts (T.V., cushioned chairs, cars, telephones, computers) in their office whereas the lowest, lower and the lowest low, and so on, have not even a seat to sit down. The solution to such departmetal neglect of the bottom level police administration may be enforcement crimes;

4. Lack of confidence and trust among the personnel employed at various ranks and too much of attachments with political higher ups, socially better off and economically affluent, and so on. According to some, the departmental contacts may disown them while extradepartmental contacts may save them when they are in trouble. As they maintain affiliations, attachments and affinities with extradepartmental points and persons, they have no option but to commit enforcement crimes just to maintain their continued contacts with such extradepartmental forces.

I got in touch with senior and very senior police officers and asked them to speak out the reasons for the continued existence of enforcement crimes. They advanced many causes and crackpot theories and some of them were:

1. Lack of leadership

2. Lack of loyalty
3. Political interference
4. Co-operation among like-minded officers/men to make fortunes by involving in enforcement crimes
5. Lack of moral sense and values
6. Lack of commitment in police work—rather having greater interest to make fortunes within the shortest time possible.

A full and perfect picture about the extent and intensity of the enforcement crimes and their causes could not have been obtained unless I collected the views and opinions of the general public on the issues. They vociferously said that enforcement crimes are rampant in police department. They brought forward many reasons and a few of them were:

1. Lack of civic culture and citizens/public servants responsibility.
2. Lack of values and respect for human dignity.
3. Ego inflation/swelling and a feeling that they can do anything without being afraid of anybody/anything.
4. Sweet-heart contracts and secret understanding with politicians, affluents and influentials, and so on.
5. Lack of public resistance to enforcement crime. Public tolerance/encouragement, etc, for enforcement crimes. Lack of supervision and surveillance.
6. Weakness of top and middle level administration, etc.

A few retired police officers/men were asked to tell openly their views on enforcement crimes. They said:

1. Interpersonnel rivalry and hostility
2. Unethical affiliations and political exploitations
3. Politician-police-businessmen nexus

4. Dearth of police administrators with leadership qualities
5. Selfism, selfishness, exploitation, fortune making, culturelessness, etc.

Enforcement Crimes and Police in the Twenty First Century

People now know all types of enforcement crimes that take place in police culture/department. The people and the press/media have started reacting to the enforcement crimes committed by police. How to remedy the situation becomes, therefore, a matter of paramount importance. Inculcation of a work culture with desirable personality traits and commitment may be an option. How to achieve the objectives? I contacted police officers/men and asked them to suggest ways and means to achieve the objectives. Some of the suggestions were as follows:

1. Inculcate the value that it is only through hard and committed work, one can reduce enforcement crimes.
2. Members of the police service must acknowledge the fact that the name and fame of the department lie in the hands of every member of the service. Each one must recognize that police is a service and the service can be given only if one has the aptitude, attitude and inclination towards the same.
3. Police is a man-oriented service and faithfulness/ truthfulness is the root of foundation of success in police service. One must be honest to himself, to others in the department and to the people in society.
4. Ego feelings, status consciousness, authority, etc, should not be the causes for enforcement criminality. Abuse of authority and misuse of power must have no place in police functionings. Every police officer/man has responsibilities, obligations and duties. They must be exercised in accordance to the expectations of the people who are the

patrons of police in a democracy.

5. Who is big-bigger-biggest in service or in society should not influence one when he exercises his power and authority. The power and authority are given to ensure just justice and nothing more.

6. Be punctual to work and show honesty in everything. Do not postpone the work or hoard the files. Be decent and dignified in the work entrusted.

7. Honour the dignity of people—dignity of time—dignity of issues and dignity of police job. Be dignified in thoughts, words and actions.

8. Be a model to others. Each one from constable to the directorgeneral, is a model to some one. People see how one behaves and they make judgements. This thought must influence every one when he does a work. In police work, everything is transparent to some one. Things that were done in darkness have come out to day light. Custodial deaths that had taken place decades ago come out for discussion and decision.

9. Be service minded. There is no substitute for it. In the name of service or in the pretext of offering service, never venture to do injustice to any one. The helpless, the oppressed, the downtrodden, the dejected, the depressed and the forsaken approach police for service. Enforcement crimes done to them may be unknown to many but they decide the justness and efficiency of the department.

10. "I am always right" and "the king commits no crime"—these attitudes and approaches have paved the way for many types of enforcement crimes. There is a greater greatness in the greatness of thinking *"errare humanum est"*—i.e., to err is human and the impact is less of enforcement crimes.

11. Respect the superiors and honour the subordinates. Accept the limitations and acknowledge the strength of others. No one is worse than any one. Every one has some inherent goodness in him and is a mixture of good and bad.

Thus, any number of suggestions can be obtained from the members of the police service to improve their performance and to bring down enforcement crimes. Police administration through everyone's participation will yield better results and will guarantee richer dividends during the 21st century-in the third millenium.

I know that many in police service have concrete suggestions to make for eliminating enforcement crimes in the service. But, they are not given opportunities and stages to speak out what they are having in their mind. I know that there are many (in police service) who make conscious attempts not to indulge in the commission of enforcement crimes. But, they are not projected out. I know that there are many who want to improve the police service, but their voice is not heard. The impact has been that enforcement crimes continue to take place in police culture and hierarchy.

References

1. E.H. Sutherland and D.R. Cressey, *Principles of Criminology,* 9th ed. J.B. Lippincott Co., Philadelphia, 1974.

2. James Vadackumchery, *Management Thoughts on Police Administration,* A.P.H. Publishing Corporation, Delhi, 1998.

3
TRAINING AND MANAGEMENT

Enforcement crimes are not unique to police department. They are seen in all government departments, from A to Z: agriculture to zoo and museums, but the visibility of the enforcement crimes in police is greater than what they are in other departments. In the World Cup Cricket, some one jumped to the court and spoke indecently to Indian Cricketers. Immediately, police rushed to the spot and took the miscreant into custody. India was defeated by South Africa on that day and many people who saw the match in the mini-screen asked: "Why?, What happened? Why the policeman?" Nobody could answer the question and many people waited for the next day's paper to know what happened in the Hove stadium in England. Some got in touch with the paper offices and the viewers of the match said: "Look at the policeman. How calmly and unemotionally he is handling the situation?". It means that everything the police do are very conspicuous and people make opinions. Any enforcement crime committed by policemen in public will be adversely commented. In one instance, people noticed that stones were kept in a police vehicle kept at a scene of law and order disturbance and the interpretation was that they were stored in the police vehicle just to stone at the aggressive crowd if that was necessary. Whatever that be, there is a view that enforcement crimes have their origin in recruit-ment—recruitment of unworthy candidates to police service.

Recruitment and Enforcement Crimes

I have given lectures to bank officials on bankers' safety in money transactions and invariably I used to ask a question: "when does a bank fraud start" and the answer used to be "from the moment an account is opened by a customer". Yes, it is true. The one who wants to commit fraud on the bank plans it when he opens an account. Hence, the bank manager takes all precautions to ensure his identity and he insists that some one known to the bank must introduce the newcomer to the bank. In spite of those precautions, frauds are committed. That is another side of the story.

Enforcement crimes, I think, have a beginning in the defective process of recruitment to police service. All police commissions including the National Police Commission did write a chapter on recruitment. The Central Committee on police training made specific recommendations to have psychological screening of candidates to police departments. The recruiting agency has to devise and design special psychological tests for the purpose. As far as my information goes, Indian police has not so far devised any dependable and reliable psychological tests for the purpose. Why? There is no answer to the question. The answer is that there is the purposeful unwillingness to do so. Are we so incapable to do so ? Are we so poor to do so? Do we lack technical expertise to do so? No. Never. Then, where has the matter gone wrong? If India could make enviable achievements in space researches, telecommunication areas, transport, agriculture and scientific inventions, certainly we can devise and design valid psychological tests for the purpose. We have money, technical expertise, manpower and above all urgent need. Yet, nothing is done in the area. The impact has been that people with undesirable personality traits and enforcement crime—prone tendencies creep into a man—oriented service. The roots of enforcement crimes are doubtlessly in the defective process of recruitment.

People have taken note of widespread corruption and political interference during the recruitment of candidates to police service. There was a time when the recruitment was undertaken by the police department. The impact of public reaction to police recruitment by police officers paved the way for entrusting the job to the public service commissions in some States. The public service commissions too conduct the tests and select the candidates to police service in a traditional way. Physique and intellegence are taken into account by measurements and tests in a conventional manner and little or very liltle emphasis is given to make a psychological screening of candidates in an objective way. Candidates who have undesirable personality traits and defective social outlooks do a lot of damage to the service—nay, cause havoc in administration of justice and enforcement of law by indulging in the commission of enforcement crimes. Candidates with higher educational qualifications may be intelligent people, but intelligence alone does not and cannot ensure desirable personality traits.

Physique, intelligence, education, psychological qualities and personality play a role in law enforcement and justice administration. So long as all of them are not taken into serious consideration, then it is virtually difficult to bring down the extent and intensity of enforcement crimes. I have asked many new entrants to police to tell me honestly the reason why they opted for police job. Their responses were:

1. No other job, hence the police job.
2. No better job, hence the police job.

Of course, this does not mean that all join the police service as constables because of the reasons shown above. It means that many who do not have the right aptitude and service-mindedness accept police job. After the enlistment as constables, they understand more about the nature of police job and the lack of promotions, etc. They feel desperate and thereafter they make attempts to make an "earning" from the job. Thus, they drift into the commission of enforcement crimes which ensure to them some satisfaction, money and fortune. They find many who experience similar tensions, frustrations and difficulties. They live in a sub-culture which accepts, tolerates, encourages some forms of enforcement crimes. By learning, association and other processes, they too become a part of the sub-culture where enforcement crimes are seen in many ways. In a South Indian State, constables are recruited to the armed battallions. After a period of time, they are eligible to get a transfer to the district armed reserves. There, they will become the juniormost among the constables. Why do they forgo their seniority and promotion prospects in armed batallions? The reason is that their entry to the armed reserve as the juniormost makes them eligible to move to the general executive branch in Thana Police. After a period of time, the constables in armed reserves can opt for an entry to the local police (general executive branch). But, again they become the juniormost among the constables in the general executive branch. Yet they do so. Why?

I have asked many constable brethren to tell me honestly about the motive behind their desire to join the local police (general executive branch) even by forgoing their seniority and promotion prospects. In that State, at present the promotion prospect of the constabulary in battallion is brighter than what is seen in the local police. Their responses were:

1. To make an earning along with their salary.
2. To enjoy some advantages, perks, privileges, comforts, power and authority through their frequent contacts with the general public.

I have observed that the constables employed in the general executive branch enjoying better life comforts than their fellow colleagues who work in armed battallions (examples: costly dress, etc.) and I used to ask myself how could they manage to have them during a short spell of time they worked in the general executive branch. Of course, there may be any number of explanations justifying their income and earnings, yet behind their explanations, justifications and rationalizations, one can find a variety of enforcement crimes.

This is a time when campus recruitment is seen in India. The intention behind such campus recruitment may be to get the best candidates at a younger age. Their purpose is to recruit the best "human machines" for efficiency and they succeed in their attempts. But, police is a man oriented—people oriented—democracy oriented—service oriented—justice oriented—enforcement oriented—public facility for the people. Precisely therefore, the recruitment must be qualitatively—human quality—better than the recruitment to a factory or production centre. Hence, every attempt must be made to screen candidates having desirable personality traits and human qualities. Psychological tests must be administered to ensure the qualitative efficiency. Being a public facility which has constant interaction with the public, opportunities to involve oneself in the commission of enforcement crimes are maximum in police service.

Entry to the level of sub-inspectors needs to receive more attention now. There too, no psychological tests are purposively and meaningfully administered. The impact is that the human quality of candidates having the right aptitude for police service may not come in large numbers to police department. The attitude, aptitude and good personality traits develop from the moment a child is born and they get matured as they grow older and older.

Anybody can function as a police officer in the traditional concept of policing provided he is given the required training. Is it enough to have such police officers? No. A sub-inspector who is the kingpin in a police station—being an officer working at the cutting edge level—must have human qualities and values. Does the recruitment procedure today ensure the entry of right candidates with right attitude and an upright conscience? If not, something must be done at the recruitment stage itself to guarantee the enlistment of candidates having right attitude aptitude, and personality traits.

Police commissions and research studies bring out the inadequacies in the recruitment processes. But, their suggestions and recommendations do not receive administrative attention and follow up actions. I have asked senior police officers to speak to me the reasons why the administration fails to implement these constructive suggestions? They say that any proposal made to the Government in this regard is evaluated by the civil staff in the secretariat and they turn down the proposals on some count or another. They have no information about the purpose of policing today and it is indeed difficult to convince them as they do not show a listening or understanding attitude.

Politicians and decision-makers in political party, often, like to see that some candidates of their preference and their party somehow enter the police department. Any innovation introduced with an objective to screen candidates having right attitude to police work and aptitude to police job may defeat their vested interests during recruitment. As a result, they too are not inclined to take up the matter and find solution to it.

Gore Committee, as early as 25 years ago, recommended psychological screening of candidates to police service as sub-inspectors. The recommendation remains to be a recommendation even today. No reliable and objective tests have been designed and devised. At the same time, the services of 'some' psychologists at the time of conducting the 'interview' may be made use of by the recruiting agency and that too in an "adhoc fashion". Without administering any objective psychological tests, these "psychologists" make subjective decisions about the personality traits and other psychological parameters of the candidates. The interview for a candidate lasts for a few minutes and during those short moments, a number of questions are asked by a number of people in the interview board and the "psychologists" get little or no time to make a fruitful and objective assessment of the candidates. I have asked some "psychologists" who had assisted the recruiting agencies to tell me honestly about the effectiveness and objectivity of psychological screening of candidates to police service as sub-inspectors. Some of them were candid enough to tell me that the process was more of ritualistic in nature than realistic. The psychologists themselves do not respect what they do during a selection process and then, what to speak about the objectivity, validity and reliability in the so named psychological screening.

Should we still continue the antiquated selection procedures? So far the police have not carved an enviable image in public about their services and should we allow the same image to go to the 21st century? Once a director general of police in an address to the lawyers, public men and members of the public candidly admitted that the police image was bad. Cultural projections, media coverages, research studies and people's experiences endorse the view of the director general. Having understood so much, should the police still delay objectivity in psychological screening during the selection processes? Enforcement crimes have their roots deeply gone into the defective recruitment procedures.

There is no dearth of literature on the subject. What is lacking is an administrative willingness to implement the modern concepts and techniques of recruitment. Police in other countries do them and yet the police in India keep their eyes shut to what they see outside. Where has the matter gone wrong?

In my book titled *Human Rights Friendly Police: A Myth or Reality*, I have discussed in detail the effect of defective early infancy, infancy and adult personality development in exhibiting human rights unfriendly police behaviour. The same observations are equally valid in the case of enforcement crimes in police service. Family, schools, community and society play a decisive role in the development of human personality and in the acquisition of desirable personality traits. Family has a particular responsibility for developing desirable personality traits, worth of the person and his dignity in the growing children. The schools have an added responsibility towards the same. Recruitment procedures and various tests intended for recruitment should ensure that candidates possessing human qualities are enlisted to the service. Responsible policing in a democracy is demanding and by the very fact that it is demanding, it builds up the true good of man and allows it to radiate to others. The radiating is manifested through absence of enforcement crimes in police work.

Recruitment of the officers to the level of deputy superintendents/assistant superintendents of police may be guided by principles and procedures which may help to enlist better qualified candidates to police service. In a class conducted to give special coaching to aspiring candidates to the middle level of police administration, I asked a question: "What are the values that you intend to uphold in your service as police officers?" Dishearteningly enough, I could learn that they were more concerned about their own security in life than any special values in their career. Authority, power, income, earnings, status, ego-satisfaction, ego prejections, etc, were the guiding forces for them. Of course, some of them might enter the service, but will they satisfy the aspirations and expectations of the people for whose welfare and protection they work in society?

How many officers of the senior levels have been trapped for involving themselves in the commission of enforcement crimes? They may be a legion and what remedial steps have been initiated to eradicate the malady at the stage of recruitment? Defective recruitment enlists unworthy candidates and they express their obnoxious traits all throughout their career. They may misuse their power and abuse their authority for their personal advantages basing on a utilitarian philosophy. Their programmes of utilitarianism, based on an individualistic understanding of policing, its use and misuse without responsibilities is the opposite of responsible policing in a democracy. Their perverted concept of policing when enforced in society with their power and authority, then it proves a systematic and permanent threat to social welfare and law enforcement. In this regard, one can mention many dire consequences, which can be statistically verified, even though a great number of enforcement crimes are hidden and unknown to the people who involve themselves in the commission of such enforcement crimes.

Training and Enforcement Crimes

In an interview with me by *The Hindu*, I said "A Central Police University, which can coordinate the functionings of the police training colleges in the various States, is needed if police training is to become purposeful. Such a University can set a common syllabus, conduct a common examination and award recognized degrees. Only in this way can we attract academics to the field and encourage researches.

The need for a proper faculty for training in specialized areas is also being felt. To teach human rights, for instance, the police training colleges rely on police officers, lawyers, professors and so on who may be as ignorant as the taught in these matters".[1]

Enforcement crimes are closely linked with the type of training given to policemen/officers. An entry to police training institutions give ample opportunities for the new entrants to associate themselves with many police officers/men who are in active service. In the previous chapter, the impact of association to develop enforcement crime tendencies among police functionaries has been dealt with. An incarcerated convict learns to commit crimes through his association with other convicts in prisons. Likewise, enforcement crimes are many and various. Entry training and post induction training may equip many to involve themselves in the commission of enforcement crimes particularly when there takes place a neglect in the inculcation of values among the trainees.

Police administration must decide whether or not there should be value-oriented and meaningful training for officers/men. If the administration decides that there should be effective and value based police training, then there are ways, means and methods to actualize the desires. The main purpose of training is not only to impart professional knowledge (there is no substitute for it), but also to inculcate values to the law enforcement officers. For imparting values, there should be trainers who possess values. A director general of police who was notoriously known for his unethical dealings, blameworthy character and corrupt nature came to engage a class on police ethics in an Academy. After his lecture, the participants to the training commented: "Look at the satan who accuses the sinner". Yes, the devil was quoting from Bible and the effect has been contempt towards the value he preached. There may be no effect if a prostitute accuses a sex-worker who is less active than the notorious prostitute herself. An enforcement criminal must not speak much about enforcement crimes and their eradication. It is nothing but self-deceit and deception on others.

Training and Management

'Charity begins at home'—this may be a cliche-ridden thought, yet it is meaningful. For, there is a view that enforcement crimes begin in the departments, as the breeding place of all types of enforcement crimes is found to be inside the four walls of police offices. Once a police officer said: "Many police officers are busily busy doing nothing". How to remain in service without doing any work is an art which officers/men study by observing what is going on everyday. A police officer again said: "Do not do any work, but give an appearance that you are doing wonderful work". He continued: "everything must be full and perfect on papers. You do anything as you like, but papers must be self-speaking". Of course, it is an enforcement crime, yet people do it, why?

Authority can be misused if one wants to do so. In my book titled *Departmental Inquiries and Injustice,* I have discussed in detail how far and how much did the disciplinary authorities misuse their power and authority. I am really shocked to see a number of disciplinary actions initiated on flimsy and flippant grounds, out of vengeance and hostility—at the instigation of others. I have read hundreds of judgements from administrative tribunals, high courts and Supreme Courts of India. In most of the petitions, the courts blame the departmental authorities for their alleged commission of enforcement crimes on employees.

"Human rights" of co-workers and subordinates are violated. They want to see others "less" in front of them. Some portion of a memo written by a principal of a police training college to a civilian member of the faculty is reproduced:

"You have sent a letter in a letter head with bold "Police Training College" on the top of the page (with name and designation of the *officer—this part is concealed here)* on the left side. This is quite deceptive and gives an impression that, it is an official letter of head of the police training college........................You are hereby restrained from using this letter head, which gives the impression that you are the very senior officer in police training college. You are hereby reminded once again that you are one among the six middle level officers in PTC. This is the fifth memo issued to you. If you continue to use this letter head again, I will be constrained to initiate disciplinary action against you.

Please acknowledge receipt.

Sd/-

Principal

On a close scrutiny of the case (enforcement crime), it is learnt that five memos were written by the principal to a civilian member of the faculty during a period of seven days. The principal was abusing his higher position and ultimately, he managed to see that the professor was placed under suspension. Owing to his contacts with the higher ups in police, he could see that the professor was kept under suspension for 10 months. Finally, the professor approached the High Court and had to spend a lot of money and time on that account.

'Training' police officers with 'values' is of great importance now. For, some senior level police officers still live in glass castles and they think that they can throw stones on others who work with or under them. Time has changed now a lot and they must be taught about the changes in society. Training can inculcate these changes in them. Enforcement crimes which were committed in the past (without being questioned then) are not tolerated now. Every man is born with dignity and each one is equal in dignity with others. This principle is increasingly accepted in human rights friendly policing.

Police training has many defects today and these defects may cause wrong perceptions and corresponding enforcement crimes. Police-human relations, enforcement of gender justice, victim justice, human rights justice, equal justice, enforcement justice, social justice, just justice, total justice, distributive justice, administrative justice, etc, are new areas about which the police functionaries must be well informed so that they take adequate precautions not to commit enforcement crimes against any areas in justice administration.

I have had discussions with senior and very senior police officers about gender justice. Some of them were found to speak "this and that" and I could understand that they needed further information on the subject. I have had contacts with people of the general public and I could learn that some of them were well informed of the concept of "gender justice". A lot of seminars, workshops, lectures, symposia and consultations are going on among them—outside the police department—and they look at the police from their special angles. If they see that the police violate the principles of gender justice, they interpret such police activities as enforcement crimes against gender justice. Ignorance of police officers on such matters may not be accepted as an explanation or excuse and precisely therefore complaints may be sent against police functionaries. The press and media may project such enforcement crimes against gender justice and they bring the news with their views.

Gender sensitisation and special training on gender justices to police officers may be the only remedy to the situation. A situation has now emerged that the people in society are better educated and well informed than some of the learned police officers. Such people may not allow enforcement crimes to take place in society as they used to be in the past.

Human rights justice is another area of public interest. There are a number of non-governmental organizations (NGOs) committed to promote and protect human rights. Human rights awareness programmes are continously conducted even at primary school levels and human rights clubs are organized in schools. I go to Academic Staff Colleges to take classes for college/university teachers. I learn that thay have a lot of interest to study more about human rights. The Human Rights Commissions too are investing a lot of money for creating human rights consciousness among the people. More of human rights consciousness among the people means more of chaining/handcuffing of police. A certain police officer told me that the police have the power to handcuff people but they can not as a result of human rights consciousness; nevertheless, people and the human rights activists handcuff the police in many ways.

Human rights violations are, no doubt, enforcement crimes. If "human rights consciousness" is developed at the same rate at which it is now ramified or percolated, certainly the police will be handcuffed from involving themselves in enforcement crimes against human rights. Police training institutions have no option other than educating police officers/men about police, people and human rights. Just recently, a batch of trainees complained to me that the human rights activists/media men do not allow them to turn left and right while they enforce law or investigate crimes. They also endorse the view that the police can not but become more scientific and psychological in their approaches and attitudes. People photograph the police doings/misdoings and in some cases, they videograph the entire police actions, inactions and overactions. What can the police do if the people behave the way they do? The enforcement crimes will have a natural death in due course and more of scientific policing may come into being.

How much money or funds is expended today to conduct research in police? Certainly it is not much. A situation has now emerged that the police is compelled to spend a lot of money for research and development. It has become a *conditio sine qua non* for the existence and survival of police in an enforcement crime-free way in Indian democracy. I happened to listen to a private coversation which a retired director general of police had with some of his colleagues when he went for his regular morning walk. He spoke as if he did great things, but a listener today would simply comment that all his doings then were misdoings and enforcement crimes. Training and education are the only ways by which the police officers can be informed about the latest developments in science, technology and thoughts on policing in an enforcement crime—free manner.

In my books, *Third Millennium Police: Take off Trends in India*, and also in *Indian Police and Equal Justice Under Law*, I have discussed various types of 'justices' that may lead the police during the 21st century. Enforcement crimes that the police have been committing in each area of justice—victim justice, social justice, equal justice, just justice, etc,—administration will be checked. Not only that, the police who are responsible to committing crimes will be forced to pay compensation to the victims of abuse of power and authority. As it is today, training is relatively a neglected area and precisely therefore more attention must be paid to that area for equipping police personnel on the changing milieu in justice administration.

Enforcement Justice and Enforcement Crimes

Victim justice in police is widely discussed. It is in this area the use of third degree methods, concoction of evidence, harassment of victims of crime and witnesses, political affiliations and consequent injustice done to victims, etc, come for discussion. There is a view that victim is a neglected person in police sub-culture although the police do many things to administer justice to the suffered victims. A superintendent of police just told me that one ought to consider the victims of crime as the most affected people by the commission of crime. Nevertheless, he has ample evidence to show that some unscrupulous police officers/men are not disinclined to involve themselves in committing enforcement crimes. Some such enforcement crimes are:

1. Acceptance of bribe from the victims.
2. Compelling victims to provide vehicles/fuel for vehicles for investigation.
3. Neglecting serious and sustained investigation.
4. Treating the victim as nobody owing to influences from politicians/affluent people.
5. Refusing to understand victims and to show sympathy, consideration or emotional first aid, etc.

Victims of police inaction and lethargy may be many. In communal violence and political tension, etc., the role played by police may be a cause for creating victims of violence and tension. Police can work as an effective control mechanism and conversely enough their failure/refusal to do so may create great havoc in victim justice administration. Hence inaction becomes an enforcement crime.

Excessive force used during a mob operation or public agitation may cause victim injustice. Police are given authority and weapons. The presumption is that they will make use of them only if they are necessary for the welfare and common good of the society. Excessive force or overaction in a given situation is considered as enforcement crimes against victim justice.

Victimization of co-workers and subordinates may be treated as crime against man and God. Initiation of disciplinary proceedings as an after-effect of hostility, jealousy, vindictiveness, etc, cannot be justified under any counts. Such a disciplinary authority is a curse of the department and democracy.

Like victim justice, there is the criminal justice and the police do a lot to administer criminal justice. In criminal justice administration, a lot of allegations are made against the police. This aspect is discussed in detail in the chapters that follow. Just justice system does not and can not remotely accept enforcement crimes against the criminals/suspects/accused. Police must administer justice in a just way and in such a system, there is no scope for an unjust administration of justice. Delay in administration of justice, acquittals in criminal cases, unjust investigation of crimes, etc, are serious enforcement crimes and they are treated in the following chapter in the book

Social justice is an area wherein the police play a role now. But, the poor, the helpless, the handicapped, the oppressed, the suppressed, the downtrodden, the weak, and so on, in society make a lot of complaints against police for their involvement of various types of enforcement crimes against them. They include:

1. Informal arrests, illegal detentions, unauthorized questionings, use of third degree methods, etc, which are used more against the poor and the downtrodden.
2. Human rights violations, disrespect to human dignity, ill-treatment, making of false promises, harassment, etc, are shown more against the poor and the handicapped than to the affluent and the influential.

Studies show that the incarcerated are of three categories, namely:

1. Those who are poor and unable to argue out their cases in the court.
2. Those who are unable to humour the police and invest huge amount of money to employ prominent lawyers to argue for them.
3. Those against whom the evidence collected may be very

strong. This category may be comparatively smaller in number than the other two categories.

Distribution of the inmates in a correctional institution on the basis of their financial position and social status may show that a good number of them come from the economically and socially handicapped clam. Why? The reason is that the policemen deal with cases in which the poor men/women are more involved than the rich and the affluent. The rich and the affluent commit crimes which may be above the reach of the ordinary policemen.

Though the commission of enforcement crimes against the poor and the downtrodden by the police may be of alarming numbers, the contribution of police in certain areas of social justice like abolition of untouchability, sati, child labour, child marriage, etc, may be worth mentioning. Of course, the participation of the people and the public support may be the reasons for success in such areas.

Police, it is alleged, commit a lot of enforcement crimes against the juveniles. Some of them are -

1. A juvenile is said to be a male under 16 years of age and a female under 18 years of age. But, whenever the juveniles are caught by the police, some unscrupulous policemen/officers threat them as adults by raising their age to above 16, if male and to above 18, if female.

2. Juveniles are treated like adult criminals and in practice they are denied of any advantages guaranteed by the Juvenile Justice Act 1986. Most unfortunately, some police officers/men do not know the provisions contained in the above Act that the juveniles in such cases are thus made victims of police ignorance.

3. There is no special juvenile wing in police and therefore policemen/officers who have little or no knowledge in juvenile psychology and special treatment to juveniles deal with them in a

layman's way. Certainly such treatments do more harm than good.

4. Juveniles are brought to adult police stations and exposed to everything in police stations just like the adults are exposed. Allegations are raised that police employ third degree methods and use inhuman and degrading treatment to juveniles including girls who are delinquent or neglected. Allegations of sexual harassment and abuse on juvenile girls are also reported against policemen/officers in some parts of the country.

In some States, the police do not take any special interest to do committed work to control juvenile delinquency. They deal with children only if some cases against them are reported. This sort of willful neglect in administration of juvenile justice is certainly an enforcement crime in police work.

Concepts on juvenile justice have changed a lot after the passing of the Children Acts in various States and the Central Children Act—1960. Juvenile Justice Act—1986 came into force after the United Nations brought out Standard Minimum Rules for the administration of juvenile justice. These new ideas and changed attitudes are not taught to police officers through inservice courses. Neglect of meaningful and purposive inservice courses may be a reason for the continuance of many enforcement crimes in police. Absence of inservice courses to update the knowledge/expertise makes them to continue their work in the old fashioned ways which may be objectionable to the people in the developing concepts of justice administration. Well designed and executed inservice courses have the capacity to make the police functionaries adequately equipped to administer just justice under an equal justice system. Good inservice courses provide intellectual capacity and a sort of "energy" to do things in the right way. The government and police administration must invest more money/fund towards modernizing police training even when the road becomes difficult or the paths become narrow, uphill and seemingly insuperable.

Disciplinary Justice and Enforcement Crimes in Police

What are the enforcement crimes committed by higher ups in the disciplinary area in police are discussed in detail in a separate chapter. The hierarchy which still believes in the traditional methods of discipline and "parade ground discipline" in all areas of interpersonnel relations work as a cause of disciplinary injustice. Modern concepts of management and management of personnel in police department are still a dark area in police administration. The traditional concepts of the orderly system and a feudal mentality in enforcing discipline among the lower levels are rejected by the bottom levels of police administration. I was once subjected to some disciplinary inquiry and the causes for the same are still unknown to me. Perhaps, the vengeance and the vindictiveness which a director general of police had towards his colleague was transferred to me as I happened to be close with his enemy. The director general of police had authority vested on him and his abuse of authority found expression in initiating an inquiry and causing harassment to me in many ways. The rich and meaningful administration of discipline within the police department must confirm to what is just and honest. This quality consists in one's capacity to live in truth and harmony with those who work under him.

In personnel management, superiors and subordinates must be so firmly united as to become one in the service. Supervisors and subordinates in the department, even though they are functionally different only in degrees, must share equally in the capacity to live in harmony for the greater efficiency of the police performance of duties. This capacity, characteristic of police service as a just justice system, has at the same time a human and an administrative dimension. It is through the human approaches that the superiors and subordinates live in "communion with many" who work for the common good of people. When the superiors and the subordinates are united by the human touches, they become one, and their union thus takes place in truth and justice and thus express the maturity proper to just administrators in police service. Police departments had/have the curse of having some superiors who miserably failed in this aspect and the result has been the commission of a number of enforcement crimes in disciplinary area in police. More about it is dealt with in a chapter on the same subject.

Police and Equal Justice Under Law

In my book *Indian Police and Equal Justice Under Law,* I have talked a lot about how best the police must ensure equal justice to people who have expectations. The police have to do justice to the criminals, to victims of crime/abuse of power and authority, to the society and to the police system itself. Do the police administer justice under an equal justice system? Some police officers are candid to admit that they do not, for, many are still not informed about the need and advantages of the distributive justice in police administration. Hence, enforcement crimes committed by police in different areas are not taken serious note of by many. The enforcement crimes committed in administration of criminal justice are extensively tackled in the chapters that follow. Here, the enforcement crimes committed by police to society is brought out first. They are:

1. Enforcement crimes by police are linked with police accountability to the people individually and collectively. Statistics on acquittals of criminal cases may show that more cases are acquitted by courts of law. Every acquittal defeats the ends of criminal justice and the money invested by the people becomes a waste. Are the people in India so rich to waste so much money for nothing?—for a police exercise in futility? No study has been conducted to know the exact amount of money spent on each case that has culminated in an acquittal. If the amount is calculated, certainly, it may be in several crores and the agency responsible for it is not made accountable to anybody. Sometimes, disciplinary inquiries may be initiated against officers responsible for acquittals. Does it mean anything for the loss caused to the people?

2. False cases are registered and innocent people are persecuted. The courts acquit them after a trial. What is the advan-

tage the people have in such miscarriage of justice? What is the remedy? If at all the victims of such abuse of power and authority get adequate compensation to their loss and sufferings, does it exempt the police from the liability for the misuse of manpower, resources and fund for the purpose? Misuse of the government machinery and consequent loss caused to the public exchequer, no doubt, are enforcement crimes which the police may not commit, but for their authority and the lenient attitude shown to them by the society.

3. Transfers and posting not motivated by public interest of administrative efficiency may be an enforcement crime committed by authority. Instances are plenty to show that police officer are transferred several times during an year and the intention may be to get political mileage for the ruling party in power or for pecuniary advantage for those who are transferred out or those who effect the transfer. People in society become victims of such unjustifiable transfers.

4. Delayed response to public calls or overenthusiastic actions for political advantages for the ruling party are enforcement crimes. Police still consider that it is the coercive weapon of the governments that come into power from time to time. The idea that the police is a public service facility does not, somehow or other, go deep into police subculture of behaviour. The 'fiat' attitude shown to politicians whims and fancies has caused irrepairable damages to public trust and confidence on police impartiality of justice.

5. Policing the society with people's participation is an accepted strategy today. Law enforcement via public co-operation and consensus is appreciated better in a democracy. In crime investigation, it is necessary to get public support and willing co-operation. However, the police so far could not achieve it. Why? There is the immediate need for an attitudinal change among police functionaries. Any attempt or approach not intended to acquire public support becomes an enforcement crime in police work.

6. Police officers/men are accused of misusing police vehicles and public fund for their personal advantages. It the accusations are correct, then they are violation of public trust and abuse of public money for individual purposes. Certainly, they are enforcement crimes against society. Policing is a commitment for the welfare of the people and misuse/abuse of public fund for personal benefits is a fraud committed on the people. It is alleged that the loss to the public by the commission of this sort of frauds on people comes to be several crores-perhaps, more than the loss caused by individual thieves, burglars, pick pockets, and so on, individuals in society.

Enforcement crimes committed by police to the police system may be many and some of them are:

1. Violation the code of conduct ;
2. Unfair police behaviour ;
3. Behaviour against police ethics ;
4. Disrespect shown to police uniform and salute ;
5. Disloyal to police service ;
6. Disservice to fellow colleagues ;
7. Defeat of the objectives of the system ;
8. Insincere to obligations and commitments.

Thus, one may notice that any enforcement crime is a violation of responsible policing and caring concern to society. Police in communion with other sub-systems of justice must be sensitive to their manifold duties. The foundations of the police rests on responsible policing and it can be ensured only by an upright consicience and concern for the people—criminals—victims of crime/abuse of authority/power, —to the justice system—to the society under an equal justice system.

Reference

1. M. Harish Govind, "Meet Dr. James Vadackumchery", *The Hindu,* Monday, Nov. 9, 1998.

4

ACQUITTALS IN JUSTICE ADMINISTRATION

Failure of police cases before courts of law has become a matter of grave concern and anguish for the people of India. Year after year, the conviction rate in criminal cases comes down and correspondingly, the acquittal rate goes up. This disturbing trend makes the people to lose their trust on the justice system in general and in police organization in particular. There is a view that the predominent cause of acquittals in criminal cases may be the defects in police working. Of course, the police officers/men object to it; yet behind the public's feelings, there may be some truth as well.

People get irritated at the working of the police system and the way the system works. As per the law, the police may be the sole sub-system empowered to investigate crimes. Investigation means a probe into for finding out the truth and in that probe there are many steps/procedures. Each step can be fairly executed and also performed in an unjust or foul manner. Whenever foul methods or unjust strategies are applied, there come enforcement crimes.

How Must a Crime be Investigated

Can a crime be investigated without committing an enforcement crime? This is a question put to investigators of crime and the answer is often "no crime can be investigated and the criminal brought to justice without committing an enforcement crime of some sort or another". If that is true, then enforcement crimes become necessary evils in administration of justice. If the answer is not true, then why do investigators commit enforcement crime to administer justice? Some people say "various techniques of investigation which would seem to help the police for administering justice and which are used with this intention actually open the door to adverse criticisms against police and mistrust on police way of doing things". Apart from the fact that the enforcement crimes committed by police during investigation are legally and morally unacceptable, the strategies adopted by police have a high degree of failure subsequently. A scrutiny of the judgements pronounced by courts may show that some of the enforcement crimes committed by police were solely responsible for acquittals of criminal cases. Any number of examples can be quoted:

1. In a sensational case, an investigating officer wanted to prove that the suspect was present at the scene of crime. He collected a glass and he gave him tea in the glass. The suspect took the tea leaving his finger prints on it. Later, he presented the glass containing finger prints as if it were located from the scene of crime. This was certainly an enforcement crime.

2. In one case, a girl of 15 years of age was taken into custody. Her age was written as 19 to escape from the restrictions of law contained in Juvenile Justice Act—1986. This was an enforcement crime.

Why do the police do so? There are justifications and rationalizations for their acts—but in all cases they are done to make the police strategies perfect and legally admissible. They think that they are winning the case, but in reality, they cause great damage to police reputation and public trust on police. They try to justify such enforcement crimes by claiming that the purpose of doing them is for public good and administration of justice. But, in fact, they defeat the very purpose as ultimately the cases are acquitted by courts. The number of cases acquitted on the basis of manipulated or concocted evidence may be more than the same convicted on such false evidence and witnesses. From the time a case is registered, people watch and see how it is investigated. Administration of justice starts at that point and the administration of justice is neither that of the police nor of the suspects in crime. Just justice means justice administered legally and as per law and procedure established by law.

Police is a sub-system that investigates crime and detects crime-doers. Dishearteningly enough, the detection rate in some States is deplorably low. According to the statistics provided by the National Crime Records Bureau, Government of India, property worth Rs. 99,670 lakh was stolen in the country during 1996. Nevertheless, property worth Rs. 28,142 lakhs could only be recovered. It formed 28.24 per cent to the property lost. In Manipur, the recovery percentage was as low as 4.9. Chart-1 gives detail of the value of property stolen and recovered (1986-1996) in the country.[1]

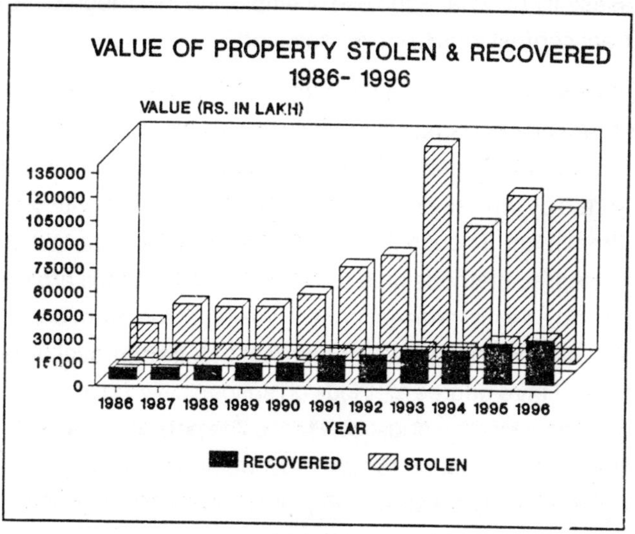

CHART-1

The recovery percentage during the decade was, however, observed to be highest at 34.7 in 1986 and lowest at 15.6 per cent in

1993—says NCRB. If the detection rate is so, it means that the investigation is poor and perfunctory. The police here finds it extremely difficult to convince the people and the press about the worth and need of police investigation in criminal cases. The causes for the prevailing and deteriorated situation may be many, but solutions are what the people want now. The people invest crores of rupees on police expecting enviable output—but the output is dishearteningly disappointing.

Can entorcement crimes find a solution to the problem? Some police officers think that property offenders usually make a confession if and only when they are interrogated in depth, i.e., by the use of third degree methods. They fail to understand that a confession does not make everything in crime investigation. Can third degree methods be a substitute for scientific evidence? Confessions may lead to recovery. But, can recovery alone lead to conviction in criminal cases? If not, what is the use of employing third degree methods to extract confessions from the accused?

Nowadays people want that the rights of the suspects must be respected and honoured. Why did such a situation come into being? People saw that a number of innocent people were manhandled and persecuted by the use of third degree methods for extracting confessions from them. Though the people may reluctantly permit the use of third degree methods on a real criminal, the people are not prepared to do so with innocent ones. Looking at the harm done to the innocent, the people in their wisdom find that disapproval of the employment of third degree methods on suspects—innocent as well as real—is administration of justice. Hence, the people all over the world accepted the law that no torture must be employed to extract confession from the suspects in crime. Any torture employed by police is considered as an enforcement crime.

The blame for employing torture on suspects falls on the pre-independent police predecessors who had promoted and approved third degree methods to prove crimes. But, history proved that the methods did more harm than good to the welfare of the people and society. No less serious responsibility for the use of third degree lies with all those officers (after independence of India till today) who encouraged the spread of an attitude of torture-permissiveness and a lack of self esteem for police department. Employment of torture on people is doubtlessly a most serious wound inflicted on people by the police—the very same people who ought to protect the life of people and their personal dignity.

In spite of many types of enforcement crimes committed by police—as the allegation goes—before, during and after the investigation of crimes one notices a consistently declining rate of conviction in criminal cases. I made a study on the issue with the following objectives:

1. To find out the trend in the rate of convictions and acquittals in criminal cases.
2. To understand the state of affairs in detection of criminal cases and its impact on people's trust upon police efficiency—particularly when the conviction rate in detected cases comes down for several decades.
3. Know the convictions in criminal cases in various States in India and to pinpoint those States where the police have poor or very poor turnouts in criminal investigation. Does the system become an unaffordable luxury for the people of India?
4. Study the percentage of convictions for offences under Special and Local laws and to appreciate the differences in trend when compared to offences under the Indian Penal Code—1860.
5. Analyse the causes of acquittal—real and judicial—and to learn the extent of accountability for the justice system for the miscarriage of justice and the right to get victimological compensation.

A question is usually asked: "How is conviction/acquittal of criminal cases correlated to enforcement crimes?". In other words: "Is there any relationship at all between enforcement crimes and acquittal/conviction of criminal cases?"

The relationship is obviously conspicuous. Every acquittal preceeds and presupposes a variety of enforcement crimes. Police cannot see that a real criminal escapes punishment without involving themselves in the commission of enforcement crimes. Innocent people surely must get themselves acquitted and in their cases, the extent and intensity of enforcement crimes will be beyond human imagination. In cases convicted by courts, who knows the extent and intensity of enforcement crimes?". How many cases are convicted on evidence honestly collected; witnesses truly produced; documents genuinely located, etc.? One who knows all those things (many more) may be able to say the extent and intensity of enforcement crimes during law enforcement.

Every enforcement crime—with the noblest of noblest motives/desires—is a crime in its real sense. I have talked to many people who got acquitted themselves from criminal courts. My doctoral dissertation was on acquittals of police cases and I understood that many (acquitted ones) had wounded hearts when they spoke enforcement crimes committed on them by the sub-systems of enforcement and justice in the country.

A consistently declining rate of convictions is a critical issue that confronts the police and the people alike today. People think that acquittals mean enforcement crimes committed against the society. Society invests a lot of money and every acquittal means waste of money to the people and loss of public trust on police. Every unjust conviction means commission of cruel enforcement crimes against people and people's trust on the justice system. Convictions must be just—justly awarded—by just means and by just people.

Data on the trial results of offences under the Indian Penal

Code 1860 is quite disturbing. Table 1 gives the trial results of IPC crimes.

TABLE 1

Trial Results of IPC Crimes[2]

	Number of Cases		
Year	*Decided by Courts*	*Convicted by Courts*	*Acquitted by Courts*
1971	301869	187072	114797
1981	505412	265531	239881
1991	667340	319157	248183
1996	843588	318965	524623

Table 1 shows that 38.2 per cent of the cases tried by courts during 1971 ended in acquittals. Why? Does it mean that the people involved in 61.98 per cent of the cases which got convicted were really culprits and others were innocent? Acquittals and convictions are taken into account only in cases which are detected and charge sheeted? What about the total number of cases reported to police? If the police are not able to detect crimes reported to them, then what is the purpose of having such a huge agency maintained at a high cost by the people?

During 1981, i.e., after 10 years, the cases acquitted had gone up to 47.46 per cent (correspondingly, the conviction was 52.54 per cent). Here too, the acquittals and convictions were taken into account from the number of cases detected, tried and judged by the courts. From 1971 to 1981, the police in India developed a lot-both qualitatively and quantitatively. If that was the claim, then what went wrong here for the low detection and conviction percentages? Police became an expensive luxury as it could not bring out expected output in crime investigation! Large-scale acquittals too ought to be treated as enforcement crimes. Police in India, however, did not take note of this deteriorated state of affairs then, or if at all, the police took note of it, they were not seriously concerned about the effect or impact of such a decline in conviction rate. No people or country could afford to spend such a huge amount of money to see that criminal cases were acquitted by courts.

In 1973, Government of India appointed a Central Committee to make recommendations to improve the system of training. It was thought that improved training methods could ensure better results in crime investigation and detection. Nevertheless, even today (1999), many of the recommendations remain yet to be implemented in a purposeful manner. The old and delapidated system continues.

52.17 per cent of the cases decided by courts during 1991 ended in acquittals (47.93 per cent were convicted). It means that the situation was further worsened from 1981. When more and more cases got acquitted, it affected adversely the public trust on police. People still hold the view that the judgements pronounced by the courts speak truth. More and more acquittals make the people to think that they can get acquittals even if they are caught by the police. Why do police investigations fail? Is it because they conduct investigation in a perfunctory manner? Is it because they do not get proper co-operation from witnesses? Is it because the prosecutors are inefficient? Is it because the laws are inadequate? The questions are more than answers and yet the fact remains that more and more acquittals mean more and more enforcement crimes.

After 5 years from 1991, the acquittal was found to be 62.19 per cent (conviction was in 37.81 per cent). Thus, during a period from 1971 to 1996, the percentage of acquittals to total number of cases decided raised from 38.02 during 1971 to 62.19 during 1996. As pointed out earlier, it may be remembered that during this period, the manpower and resources of police to perform the work more efficiently multiplied into several folds, but the net result has been quite disappointing—that there arose a credibility crisis—that the expectations of the people were very high and the success in performance by police was very low. Public trust on police capabilities to see that the offenders were punished got diminished.

In spite of the loss of public trust, the system was maintained by the people. Why? One reason is that the people are still not fully aware of this deterioration in police work. Corruption, exertion of undue influence, political pressure, disinterestedness in crime work, etc, played a role in the failure of detection and consequent reduction in convictions. In every sense, all factors and forces which worked on police to see that criminal cases were acquitted in large numbers were factors/forces responsible for the commission of enforcement crimes. The sad reality is that the conviction percentage to total crimes reported to police comes down to the level of 6-7 in some States in India. If appeals are filed it may come further down to 2-3 per cent. If this is the real picture, then it is high time that remedies and relief measures to this deteriorated situation in India are found.

Enforcement Crimes and Sub-Systems in Justice Administration

If criminal cases are investigated properly, then conviction rate can go up. A well investigated case, if tried well, certainly the acquittal rate will go down. If more and more people co-operate with the investigation, surely the police can prove the cases before the courts. Something is wrong somewhere or many things are wrong in many places. For, acquittal rate goes up. Who must be blamed for the large-scale acquittals? All sub-systems, viz. the people, prosecutor, press and the public, the defence and the court—may be contributing their share for the deplorable state of affairs. Enforcement crimes are not the monopoly of police department. A corrupt prosecutor may take a indifferent attitude to the conduct of criminal cases. The prosecutor may help the accused in many ways. The clandestine contracts between the defence counsels and the prosecutors may help to see that criminal cases end in acquittals. Nevertheless, the people generally blame the police more than they do with other agencies. The reasons are obvious. Police do a lot of work—fair or foul—from the arrest to conviction/acquittal—in connection with crime investigation and detection. Many things which the police do are conspicuously visible to the general public. The suspects/accused in crimes suffer the sufferings in connection with the investigation of crimes. They tell others about their experience in police stations and the propaganda they give carve out the image of police. The enforcement crimes they commit and the police activities interpreted by the suspects/accused as enforcement crimes may be discussed in public. Ultimately, when the criminal cases are acquitted, people look at the police in disfavour. Police and the people feel disurbed then. Some people say that the criminals are likely to escape from the court and therefore, whatever they suffer at police hands may be the real punishments—however soft or severe—which the suspects/accused interpret as enforcement crimes. There is a school of thought which argues that the acquitted must be compensated when they are set free by courts of law.

Illegal custody, informal arrests, unauthorized ways of handling the suspects and use of third degree methods, etc, as repeatedly stated earlier, are treated as enforcement crimes and the people rush to Human Rights Commissions to get compensation for the damages caused to them. Enforcement crimes are not tolerated by the public as the people consider a crime to be a crime, no matter who commits it.

Crimes are investigated by police and the expectation is that the criminals will be detected and punished. But, when the public see acquittals in large measure, they start doubting police sincerity in crime investigation *ab initio*. The present trend is to find fault with the State's machinery to the extent of demanding investigation by the Central Bureau of Investigation. Most unfortunately and dishearteningly enough, the CBI is facing a credibility crisis now as it becomes a target of adverse and negative criticisms from superior courts and the press in the recent past.

People, of late, express their lack of confidence in CBI's investigation and they emphatically say that the investigation conducted by the Nation's premier agency is in no way superior to the same conducted by the State Police agencies. They may be true in their view as the convictions in cases investigated by the CBI during 1996 too were not very enviable. The convictions in cognizable cases registered under the Prevention of Corruption Act and related sections of the Indian Penal Code were 74.57 per cent. This must be appreciated with another fact, that the conviction rate in some developed countries is as high as 98 per cent and in certain States in India, the conviction rate is higher than what the CBI has. CBI enjoys more facilities often far superior, in many ways, to the same possessed by State Police departments.

A few years ago, I conducted a study on CBI's investigation and found that the people in general were happy with the CBI But, today I do not find such happiness among people even when the CBI comes to the scene for investigation. There exists a credibility crisis although some people still insist on CBI's investigation in criminal cases. Why do the people do so? One of the reasons is that they do not have a better system. When no option is available, people make the best option by demanding CBI's investigation. People hold the view that undue influence and unnecessary political interference may be minimum with CBI when compared with the State police machinery. In some States, crimes are investigated first by the Thana Police; then by the special investigation team under the district superintendent of police; then by the Crime Investigation Branch of the State Police and then by the Central Bureau of Investigation and thus a lot of time is spent for investigation, reinvestigation, further investigation and further reinvestigation and the ordeal continues until at last the issue is closed. Thana Police may not be a specialized unit in crime investigation and if the police officers who belong to specialized investigation speak the truth, then the initial investigation done by Thana Police damages the investigation in many ways at the beginning itself. They may even contaminate the evidence and it is not just possible to arrive at right conclusions with contaminated evidence and perfunctory investigations. These sort of perverted procedures and distorted methods are nothing but enforcement crimes.

What is it to the police if criminal cases are acquitted? The police stand to lose nothing or to gain nothing—this is a very dangerous attitude which must be condemned by strongest words.

Table 2 shows convictions in criminal cases in States[3] (1996)

TABLE-2

Conviction in Criminal Cases-1996

States	Convictions (percentages)	
	IPC Offences	*Su Offences*
Andhra Pradesh	33.6	98.8
Arunachal Pradesh	52.1	62.5
Assam	22.4	37.0
Bihar	28.6	35.1
Goa	21.1	65.4
Gujarat	35.9	25.5
Haryana	47.7	60.1
Himachal Pradesh	32.9	15.5
Jammu & Kashmir	39.0	44.7
Karnataka	19.0	97.4
Kerala	27.7	55.6
Madhya Pradesh	50.9	96.6
Maharashtra	18.8	61.0
Manipur	15.4	99.6
Meghalaya	63.5	88.9
Mizoram	85.9	96.3
Nagaland	17.4	95.2
Orissa	14.5	27.9
Punjab	44.0	64.7
Rajasthan	48.9	67.0
Sikkim	72.7	94.4
Tamil Nadu	63.6	90.5
Tripura	18.3	15.4
Uttar Pradesh	50.7	78.2
West Bengal	15.2	98.7
Union Territories	39.6	56.3
All India	37.8	87.3

A doctor, while he conducted a surgery, made a mistake causing the death of the patient. He was made accountable to what he did. A vehicle driver caused an accident and thereby a passenger was killed. The driver was made accountable. A house was constructed by an engineer and it collapsed. The engineer was made accountable for what he did. If this is what is followed in many areas of human transactions, the people ask a simple question. Whenever a criminal case is acquitted by a court of law, why can't the subsystems responsible for the same be made accountable? A closer analysis may show that the acquittal is the result of many enforcement crimes committed by agencies responsible for administration of justice.

The people in a democracy place their full confidence on their agencies for administration of justice. The State takes up the responsibility to investigate crimes and to bring the offenders to justice. The people invest a lot of money for the purpose. An acquittal means miscarriage of justice and no society invests its hard earned money for miscarrying justice. Hence the agencies responsible for the same must be made accountable for what they do. Every unsuccessful prosecution is a failure of the justice system and the failure has occured owing to the commission of enforcement crimes by an agency, then the responsibility and accountability for the same must be fixed on the agency.

Just see the percentage of convictions in various States. 14.5 per cent of the offences under IPC tried by courts in Orissa during 1996 ended in convictions. In West Bengal one may see 15.2 per cent. In Nagaland, Tripura, Manipur, Maharashtra, Karnataka, etc, the percentage of conviction was less than 20. The issue under discussion is: "How far or how long can or should the people afford to tolerate this deplorable situation?. If it is not the people (a faceless mass) who invests money, how long can the system producing such a low output be maintained? No invester can afford the luxury when proper turn out is not guaranteed by the system. For example, people invest a lot of money for educating their children. But, if they see that the students studying in a particular school/college fail in large numbers, they may think of winding up the institution even by terminating the teachers. Private companies see to it that the employees are sent out by the principle of Hire and Fire when they find that the output is not enviable. Management by objectives is an accepted theory in all walks of life including justice administration. When expected results are not produced, one cannot maintain an unaffordable luxury. Applying the same principle in law enforcement and justice administration, people today place a lot of expectations on their police, prosecutors and courts.

Investigation of a cognizable crime is something which the police alone can do and if they fail in their duty, then no one can justify the activities of the sub-system. As the state of affairs is today, all crimes are not reported to police. Only a few crimes reported to police are detected. Elsewhere, it has been pointed out that the detection in property stolen has come down to 15.6 per cent during 1993. In some States, it has never crossed 30 per cent at any time after India became independent. If this is the reality, what does the low percentage of convictions show?

If the criminals feel that they can commit crimes without being detected, surely it gives an incentive for some of them. The lifelong earnings of a person is lost just in a moment and the States machinery is helpless to detect the criminal. Even in such desperate moments, the people retain the sub-system by huge investment and nobody is accountable.

All cases detected by police may not be sent for trial. As discussed earlier, when conviction rate is computed on the basis of total crimes reported it may be shockingly noticed that the conviction percentage lowers still down. Allegations are there that the police, sometimes, simply refuse to register criminal cases if they do not find possibilities of detection. In some cases, political interference and affluent introductions become necessary even for registering criminal cases! Both fall under enforcement crimes in police service. If the police refuse to register criminal cases, what is the alternative. The victim of offences may have to approach higher ups in police or to prefer a complaint before the court of law. Even in such cases, ultimately the investigation will be entrusted to police. It being so, the ordinary man in the street thinks three times whether or not he must go up in the hierarchy with complaints or prefer a complaint directly to the court of law. Human element in investigation of crime is important and as such an investigation entrusted to police from above may be unpleasantly investigated with little or no commitment in further progress? Policemen/officers now claim that they are professionals in investigation and precisely, therefore, they must show professionalism in inspection, interrogation, interviewing and instrumentation. These four I's in investigation are important and any indifference or neglect in implementing them in a professional manner may affect adversely the result of crime investigation. Responsibility falls on police investigators to conduct investigation in a professional manner and any laxity in doing so may be treated as an enforcement crime. Of course, the police can manage and manipulate things to their favour and therefore a specific and no less serious responsibility lies with superiors and still superior ranks. If they do not do so, then they show an encouraging attitude to enforcement crimes and a lack of esteem for just justice.

Enforcement *Mens Rea* and Enforcement Crimes

Mens rea is a known concept in criminal jurisprudence, but enforcement mens rea is a novel concept. I introduce it to criminal jurisprudence. As everyone knows what is mens rea, there is no need to hold a discussion on the concept. Nevertheless, enforcement mens rea is not known to many. Usually, police officers say that they employ third degree methods (enforcement crime) not for any personal advantage or for obtaining any individual mileage. It is done for public good and thus they try to justify the enforcement crime they commit. They argue so, because they want to say or establish that they have no mens rea when they commit such enforcement crimes. Of course, individual achievement may not be there in using third degree methods, yet there is achievement for the department. If a crime is proved or a confession is obtained by means of third degree method, the status and prestige of the police department may be increased. The news may be flashed in the media and the department gets a fame and name.

Some police officers may produce tutored witnesses (enforcement crimes) to prove the cases before the courts of law. There too, they do so to get name for the department. The argument is that commission of certain kinds of enforcement crimes by police is to bring name and prestige for the police department. If that is so, the department has to own the responsibility for the commission of enforcement crimes. The *mens rea* is then for the department and therefore I wish to call it "enforcement *mens rea*". If the department can enjoy the merit obtained by the commission of enforcement crimes by individual members, let the department take up the burden of shouldering the demerits of committing enforcement crimes.

The argument of the department may be in a different line. After all the department has not entrusted any of its members to commit enforcement crimes. If any one does so, it is at the personal risk of the individual police officer/man. Hence the department can not own the responsibility for the same. As such, there is nothing called "enforcement *mens rea*". Why should a police officer risk his career for making fame for the department? Whatever may be the arguments, the corporate responsibility of police officers/men leads to a new concept known as "enforcement *mens rea*". In other words, it is a "corporate *mens rea*"—a new concept that is being developed in the west in recent past.

There may be cases in which only the investigating officers alone get personal advantage by committing enforcement crimes. In such cases, there may not be any *enforcement mens rea*. Such cases must be dealt with on a different footing.

Enforcement mens rea and the commission of enforcement crime are closely linked. One can not exist without the other. Therefore, accountability to enforcement crimes must be fixed both on the department and on police department.

What are the conviction—percentages in special and local laws in India? In some States, the conviction—percentages are better when it is compared to the Indian Penal Code. In States like Manipur (99.6 per cent), Andhra Pradesh (98.8 per cent), Karnataka (97.47 per cent) Madhya Pradesh (96.6 per cent), Nagaland (96.1per cent) and West Bengal (98.7per cent), the percentages of conviction under special and local laws are enviably high. However, such States do not show a similar trend in IPC offences. For example, the position in West Bengal is 15.2 per cent (IPC) and 98 per cent (SLL); in Tripura 18.3 per cent (IPC) and 90.5 per cent (SLL), in Orissa 14.5 per cent (IPC) and 95.2 per cent (SLL) and finally in Manipur 15.4 per cent (IPC) and 99.6 per cent (SLL). What is the reason for an unbelievably high percentage of convictions for offences under special and local laws whereas they are unimaginably poor for offences under the Indian Penal Code? Where exactly are the defects/merits present?

The same police officers investigate crimes under Indian Penal Code and the Special and Local Laws. Yet, the percentages of conviction are higher for the latter. The same laws of procedure and evidence are applicable in both cases. Crime Investigation Branches, CBI, etc, investigate generally crimes under the Indian Penal Code and it is the Thana Police who often investigates offences under special and local laws. Yet, the convictions are higher. If enforcement crimes take place in the area of IPC crimes, then the chances are equal for the enforcement crimes to take place in the area of special and local laws. In spite of it, the conviction rates are higher. Why? The high percentages of conviction in special and local laws are indeed enviable and go on a par with the conviction rates in well advanced countries in the world. In some States, almost hundred per cent of the cases under special and local laws end in convictions.

Enforcement Crimes and Causes of Acquittals

Research studies have fairly well identified the causes of acquittals. Mainly, the studies concentrate on offences under the Indian Penal Code and which were investigated by Crime Investigation Branch of the State Police. The findings are equally applicable to the investigations conducted by police (other than those belonged to the Crime Investigation Branch) including the CBI.

No doubt, the police, prosecutor, witnesses, defence counsels, courts, etc, are responsible for the large-scale acquittals of IPC offences. The police blame the prosecutors for the low output and the prosecutors blame the police for the poor conviction rates. The police and prosecutors together blame witnesses for the state of affairs. Blaming each other/one another may not solve the issues under discussion. I asked police officers to tell me the crooked practices which the prosecutors employ so that aquittals are possible for the accused. A few of the important causes are:

1. Corruption and sweet heart agreements not to argue the case properly. Some prosecutors thus mint money.
2. Inertia, lethargy and indifference to study criminal cases seriously and meticulously. They do not have any interest in the case, nor do they have any personal or pecuniary advantage for being aggressively honest in the conduct of the cases.
3. Ego clashes with police investigators and too much of ego inflations make them to ignore what the police tell them about the prosecution cases.
4. Independence of prosecutors to conduct the cases with out any accountability to any one under the sun together with their ignorance in laws, procedure and conduct of criminal cases.
5. Unholy affiliations with unscrupulous politicians and consequent "fiat attitude" to political whims.

Some police officers want the old system of having police prosecutors to conduct criminal cases to be brought back for raising the percentage of convictions. However, the prosecutors are not in favour of such an arrangement which may destroy the independence of judiciary and prosecution. The police have a lot to speak against defence counsels as well and they blame them for employing crooked practices in justice administration. They too are enforcement crimes and some of the blame-worthy practices are:

1. Secret contracts and agreements with the victims of offences and witnesses. They compromise and mutually agree to support. They play "deaf and dump" games when the cases are tried in courts of law.

2. Top secret understanding with prosecutors to play many tricks and psychological games favouring the accused—for which huge amount of money may be paid to them.

3. Purchasing prosecution witnesses at a fairly high price from their markets so that they side with the defence when the cases come for trial. For this, the help may be extended by some unscrupulous police officers as well. If nothing works to the advantage of the defence, the defence may then employ *goondas* and threaten the witnesses. Instances are plenty to show such threats from *goondas* and mafia gangs.

4. In certain areas and cities, there exist organized racketeers who negotiate between prosecution and defence to come to an agreement. If their attempts do not yield good results, then they resort to coercive tactics to see that the witnesses do not go against them. In some instances, the witnesses may meet with an accident or die an unnatural death.

5. Purchasing of veteran criminal lawyers for not aiding the prosecution is another method employed by affluent

criminals. Victims of offence who have no trust on public prosecutors may employ their own private lawyers to be an aid to the prosecutor. An affluent defence may purchase such aids along with prosecutors. Right or wrong, there is erosion of public trust on the way many things take place in administration of justice. Enforcement crimes are numerous and solutions are few

Undercurrents and Enforcement Crimes

What are the undercurrents in acquittals/convictions of criminal cases? If the undercurrents are exposed, they may show an extent of how things happen in the field of justice administration. I have conducted extensive studies in the area and got my findings published in four volumes[4]. The causes of acquittals were many and various and it is not necessary to enumerate them here. Nevertheless, key witnesses turning hostile, unbelievable versions of witnesses, contradictions in the statement of witnesses, inability of prosecutors to prove that the accused really committed the offence, failure of the counsel to prove the ingredients of the section of law, production of interested witnesses, failure to conduct witness examination, etc, were found to be some of the major causes that affected the verdicts of the courts.

I wanted to know, why or how the key witnesses turn hostile to prosecution. I talked about it to police officers, lawyers, people and prosecution witnesses themselves. One may be ashamed to listen to the mockery of justice that is being administered. Some people tolerate such mockery, others suffer it and yet others encourage it. People who tolerate and encourage such mockery commit enforcement crimes. The undercurrents of witnesses turning hostile, as I understand from my discussions, may be:

1. Witnesses are made or forced to turn hostile to prosecution—sometimes with the concurrence of police, prosecutors and victims of offence.

2. Witnesses are purchased by the defence who gives coaching to them as to how they must give testimony before the courts. The prosecution/police may get a shock in such situations, but they are helpless.

3. Witnesses are threatened and coerced to become hostile to prosecution by *goondas* and mafia gangs.

There are several other methods to win over witnesses. Persuasion, appeal, craving for sympathy, etc, are some among them. The witness is made to think: "what is the advantage I derive by sending a person to the jail". Yes, no advantage. Crime has been committed and there are many reasons and justifications for the commission of crimes. The culprit is prepared to compensate the victims of crime and once the compensation is given and accepted, what is the meaning and utility in punishing the offender? Yes, there is a point in the argument and there is a morality in the whole procedure. The witnesses become convinced of the arguments and they go to the courts to turn hostile to prosecution.

A prosecution case becomes an orphan or a police baby when the accused and the victim of the offence are prepared to compromise before the trial is conducted. The police in such instances can not get the support and willing co-operation of such hostile witnesses. Added to it, some police officers enlist unwilling people as witnesses or produce tutored witnesses, false witnesses or partisan witnesses. If that is the case, the police must be blamed for their commission of enforcement crimes and for their production of such witnesses for wasting money, time and energy of all subsystems involved in administration of justice. Why should the system work in this way when every one knows that the system does not serve its objectives. The appearance or production of a witness who has decided to turn hostile to prosecution mocks at the justice system and all those who aid him/her encourage such mockery of justice. What a colossal waste indeed!

Unbelievable versions of witnesses—is another major cause for acquittals. The versions were once believed by the police and that was the exact and the sole reason for putting him/her in the array of witnesses. The questions here are:

1. Was he/she really a genuine witness who was honest?
2. Was he/she really interviewed by the police in an honest way?
3. Was he or she really extending full co-operation and willing participation in crime investigation.

If the witness was not genuine, honest or co-operative, how could he/she become a witness? What was the undercurrent in his/her production? The answer to this question may show the extent an intensity of enforcement crimes, I contacted many police officers, lawyers and prosecution witnesses to know the undercurrents in such malpractices in justice administration. The responses were shockingly revealing the undercurrents:

1. Police make some as 'witnesses' even without their concurrence and knowledge. The statements are prepared without even interviewing them. They prepare the witness testimony in the way they want—almost in a ritualistic fashion.
2. Police asks the victim of offence to produce some people to become witnesses. They produce interested witnesses, lying witnesses, hostile witnesses, etc, and in some instances, they may be false witnesses. In a court of law, they will not be able to withstand the cross examination by a learned defence counsel. They cut a sorry figure before the judge.
3. Illiterate, uneducated, rustic witnesses may be cross-examined this way and that way with all sorts of court crafts and the defence lawyers shatter the credibility of

even honest witnesses. The defence lawyers have ethical justification for everything they do for defeating the ends of criminal justice.

Some presiding officers have little or no knowledge about the dynamics of human behaviour and naturally, their ignorance may cause misinterpretation of witness testimonies. Superior courts in many appeal judgements observe the defects in such court interpretations of human behaviour and witness testimonies.

Contradictions in the statements of witnesses—is another major cause of acquittals. The undercurrents may be anything from corruption to unconscious forces which may result in making contradictions in the statements of witnesses. The lawyers know well that Indian Evidence Act 1872 heavily depends upon the oral testimony of witnesses. Precisely therefore, they try to shatter witness testimonies in several ways. For obtaining a favourable testimony, defence lawyers play many unethical games and resort to several manipulations. Police interviewing of witnesses in a haphazard manner or interview conducted by unqualified/underqualified police personnel may help even honest witnesses to make innocent contradictions before the courts.

The inability of prosecutors to prove that the accused really committed the offence is yet another cause of acquittals. Why can not the prosecutors prove the crime against the accused? The reasons may be that (1) the accused is not guilty; (2) investigation is not seriously done; (3) prosecutor just sends the case for trial without proper evaluation of evidence; and (4) prosecutor's ignorance in the subjects, etc. In all such instances, the responsibility of the prosecutor is serious and his accountability is severe. They show how enforcement crimes may take place in administration of justice.

The undercurrents in the prosecutors becoming incapable of proving the case may not be visible. I discussed this issue with prosecutors and some of them were frank enough to say that the situation would come if :

1. The prosecutors were susceptible to introductions and influences. Corruption might play a major role there.

2. Police and prosecutors were powerful blocs and therefore they could charge-sheet an accused even when the evidence against him was not strong. The power could do many things to their advantage and they could escape their superiors enquiry as to what happened to the case. They could escape from further questioning just by saying that the case was pending before the court.

3. The prosecutors knew well that their inability to prove the crime would not affect them adversely in their advancement in career.

"The prosecuting counsels fail to prove the ingredients of the section of law" and if that is the case, what is the real role of a prosecutor in criminal trials? The ingredients of law are important and if that cannot be proved successfully, then how can they send the cases for trial? Interested witnesses are produced and the intention is quite clear.

In one of my own studies, the judicial causes of acquittals were identified and pigeonholed from the judgements pronounced by courts of law. Of course, the judicial causes of acquittals as seen in the court judgements may not be the real causes that work behind the acquittals. For a judge pronounces his verdict basing on the evidence placed before him. He may not know the undercurrents or if at all he knows them, he is helpless to do anything beyond and besides the evidence before him. For example, some criminal cases were acquitted owing to:

1. Undue delay in investigation.

2. Innocent person charge-sheeted.

3. Charge is made on civil matters.

4. Charge found to be against facts.
5. Contradictions between experts and eyewitnesses.
6. Delay in the trial of cases.
7. Circumstantial evidence unbelievable, etc.

The questions here are many: "Why was the innocent person charge-sheeted?". One may find the cruel commission of enforcement crime in such situations. How could the police collect evidence against an innocent person? How could the prosecutor appreciate the evidence so advanced by the police? What type of investigation did the police conduct? What sort of supervision the departmental authorities offer? There could be many mysteries in such cases and they might point out to a fact that the authority was misused or abused by many in power and authority. What would be the compensation against the misuse of authority? Enforcement crimes must be punished and the victims of enforcement crimes should get adequate compensation for the sufferings they undergo under several counts. I suggested this idea in one of my books and the reviewer of my book, a retired director of the Central Bureau of Investigation, could not swallow the new concept. He asked: "how could it be done?". In a seminar I put forward the idea that all innocent people who get acquitted from courts of law must get compensation and for that purpose a victim fund must be raised. Many police officers objected to my suggestion and their argument was that such a procedure might necessitate very huge amounts. For, they knew well that many who were acquitted from courts would claim damages if the law permitted them to get compensation when cases were acquitted. But, I find that my suggestion is getting more and more acceptance in these days and may be implemented in the days to come.

What is this?—the charge-sheet made on civil matter—and the question is "how". How can the police and prosecutor claim that they are administering criminal justice when they charge-sheet people on civil matters? The enforcement crimes such people commit cannot be excused or pardoned. They misuse their authority and they must see their place outside the justice administration. Charge-sheeting a person on civil matters is serious crime and it shows utter disregard to human dignity and a supreme dishonour to human person.

Why did the court observe that the charge was found to be against facts? It means that people in authority can do anything as they like. Bertrand Russel once wrote: "Like any other privileged caste, they use their power for their own advantage. They are, however, in one respect worse than any other privileged caste, since it is their business to expound an unchanging truth, revealed once for all in utter perfection, so that they become necessarily opponents to all intellectual and moral progress". The charge is on one thing and the facts are quite different from what the charge is made for. No doubt, enforcement crime is committed when a charge is made against fact. Of course, there is the provision for malicious prosecution under tortious liability being initiated against the agency for its commission of enforcement crime. But, the procedure is expensive and requires inordinate time for disposal. Such victims of the abuse of power should have an actionable claim for victim compensation. The United Nations and the international community favour this view.

Convictions in Criminal Cases and Enforcement Criminality

There is a view that every conviction presupposes a variety of enforcement crimes. They say that it is just impossible to investigate a crime strictly in accordance to law and procedure established by law. There may be very convincing evidence against the suspects in a crime. At the same time, there may be some missing links in the chain of evidence. The investigator may have to weld the pieces of evidence and for it he may have to suppress some facts or suggest some falsehood. He may have to add some links or take away some links. It is humanly impossible to find out all links in the chain of evidence and in such a situation, what must be done? Can it be called an enforcement crime if an investigator shapes a case with some evidence concocted by him? Will he be morally justified in doing so? The investigator may be subjectively justified in doing so, but what about the objective and legal justification for doing so? His argument runs as follows: "If the missing links are not put, the courts are inclined to grant benefit of doubt to the accused in crimes". In a legal system which upholds the principle: "Let one thousand criminals go unpunished, no innocent man must be punished", concoction of some missing links in the chain of evidence becomes very necessary in a few cases atleast.This view is opposed by another school of thought that no civilized law will accept the concoction of missing links for the purpose of awarding punishments to a guilty accused. The advocates of this school ask: "How much evidence can be concocted for the purpose?". The question remains unanswered and the human conscience cannot be stretched to an extent that any link can be concocted if the investigator is convinced about the involvement of the suspect in a crime. The inability of the investigator to find out the missing link in the chain of evidence is a real defect in his investigation and his inability cannot be compensated by concoction which, of course, is an enforcement crime in every sense. An investigator who commits this sort of an enforcement crime may find out justifications for his act—as if he were right which he, at least under certain compelling circumstances, may acknowledge as right and legal. He must place, himself in the position of the guilty accused therefore he is likely to feel that he must respect human dignity and then, he may naturally withdraw himself from his perverted views on administration of criminal justice. Every suspect has certain rights and the investigator must recognize them. The legal system and police procedures should limit themselves to taking account of and accepting the principle in theory and practice.

References

1. Crime in India—1966, National Crime Records Bureau, Government of India, 1998.
2. Crime in India—1966, *ibid.*
3. The four volumes got published are—
   (i) Indian Police and Miscarriage of Justice
   (ii) The Police,the People and Criminal Injustice
   (iii) The Police, the Court and Injustice
   (iv) The Police, the Accused and Criminal Justice,
   A.P.H. Publishing Corporation, New Delhi.
4. Bertrand Russel, Why I am not a Christian, Unwin Paperbacks, Boston, 1982.

5

DELAY IN DISPOSAL OF CASES

Is delay in disposal of criminal cases a crime? So far, it has not been considered as a crime, rather it is taken for granted that delay is just normal. Police take a lot of time to investigate a crime, prosecution may take further time, trial may take further time and what is there to speak about the delay in time? This has been the attitude of law and administration. In a country where the rule of law prevails and not the rule of justice, it is quite possible that the system heavily depends upon the law. Of course, limitation of crimes which are not of serious nature is there in the newly enacted Code of Criminal Procedure 1973. What is the reason behind fixing such limitations? The same reason is equally valid for crimes of serious nature as well. If rule of justice necessitated the enactment of laws prescribing limitation of time, the same rule of justice is equally applicable to all sorts of crimes. As there is no law prescribing time limit for the investigation, prosecution and trial of criminal cases, the system can take any period of time for the disposal of criminal cases. This approach indeed is against the law of justice. For, there are criminal cases which are not disposed off even after ten or twelve years after the cases were registered. Ten or twelve years in a man's life is not a short period and the position gets worsened if he is punished for several years afterwards. Rule of justice may insist that the delay must be minimum and any inordinate delay in the disposal of criminal cases is an enforcement crime in every sense.

Is there something called a rule of justice governed by rule of law. Yes, there is provided the law is just as just law alone can administer just justice. Rule of justice contains human elements and human contents which I have brought out in the preface of this book. Rule of law may be devoid of, the human elements and human contents. Inordinate delay in the disposal of criminal cases means that it is rule of law which is devoid of human elements and human contents.

How long must a man suffer for a crime he has committed? Life sentence means a fixed period of incarceration and it does not mean prison life until one's death in prisons. Even in prisons, remissions are granted and thus the period of incarceration is reduced. If paper reports are true, there have been undertrial prisoners who have spent four, five or six years waiting for the trial to begin and they are set free by the courts after the trial. Is it not injustice to do so ? —or if it is not injustice, then what is it ? More about undertrial prisoners will be discussed later in this chapter.

Human tolerance to delay in investigation or trial is something which the law does not take into account. How long can a man tolerate the delay? Tolerance is a defence mechanism which may turn out to be aggression, withdrawal, etc, and in some cases to mental disorders and psychic problems. Instances of people committing suicide have been reported in the press and moreover the agony suffered by the victims of prolonged delay in the disposal of criminal cases have been studied by few researchers and journalists. Police officers and lawyers console the victims saying :" the law will take its course" and what they mean by saying thus is "to relax" and relaxing here means experiencing tension conflicts, frustrations, agony, pain and ultimately reconciling with the realities upon which they have no say or control. The law is blind and the blind law does not contain human contents. Rule of justice is widely open and it sees man as human and respects his dignity and person.

Why delay takes place? Any number of arguments can be advanced to explain the causes of delay or explain away the personal responsibility of an individual police officer for causing delay.

Delay may be convincing more for the investigators and the police hierarchy than for the ordinary man in street and particularly so when the people have no say either in shortening the delay or in extending the delay. If a police officer purposefully delays investigation, certainly he is committing enforcement crimes. There is an argument often advanced to justify the purposeful delay and that is almost like this : "police investigators are overburdened with workload". According to the latest statistics provided by the National Crime Records Bureau, Government of India, the workload of an investegating officer in India 60.4 cases during an year i.e. 18.7 I.P.C. cases and 417.77 cases under Special and Local Laws. In some States, the workload per investigating officer is heavier than the national average. In Andhra Pradesh, it is 187.7 and in Gujarat, it is 124.2. Karnataka has 244 cases per police investigators and Tamil Nadu has 149.9 cases per police investigator. There are many States having less workload than the national average. Arunachal Pradesh (7.2), Assam (16.3), Bihar (15), Goa (22.1), Haryana (32), Himachal Pradesh (18.3), Jammu and Kashmir (12), Kerala (50.3), Maharashtra (46.4), Manipur (9.7), Meghalaya (4.2), Mizoram (8.1), Nagaland (5.4), Orissa (13.3), Punjab (6.9), Rajasthan (37.2), Sikkim (6.1), Tripura (5.2), Uttar Pradesh (52.4), West Bengal (58) are having the workload shown in brackets.[1] Yet, there takes place delay during investigation. Why? In spite of the investigation in a slow and delayed manner cases are getting acquitted in large numbers. I have discussed in detail in the previous chapter about acquittals as enforcement crimes. I want to say that an investigation done in a slow and delayed manner does not guarantee convictions from courts of law. Then what is the advantage of having so much delay in crime investigation? I ask this question because some police investigators advance arguments saying that delay ensures perfection in investigation. Hurried investigation in usually perfunctory and certain amount of delay in investigation is necessary to ensure perfection in the work and satisfaction to the victims of offence. All said and done, cases are acquitted in an alarmingly high rate.

Heavy workload, I agree, affect the quality of investigation as the police officer cannot make sustained investigation. Already allegations are heard against some police officers that they register an FIR prepare the scene and write three or four case diaries and then forget about it for a long time. In the meantime, they may register other cases and do the same exercises. If they get a transfer, then they tie everything together and escape from there. The newcomer has to study the old and pending cases. He has to register new cases and to do many other works connected with police. The rituals are thus going on until at last someone thinks of "clearance exercise" on pending cases and crime investigation. Case diaries are written, witnesses are questioned, recoveries are effected and final reports are prepared within no time and afterwards? Afterwards, cases may be acquitted. The disposal comes after five or six years after the commission of crimes and I do not know what is the earthy use or effect of such delayed verdicts of acquittal or conviction as the case may be.

Delay and Disposal of Cases by Police

An extract from *Crime in India,* 1996 is reproduced:

"During 1996, at All India level, a total of 21,66,618 cases including those pending from the previous year were awaiting disposal or investigation by police. In terms of percentage, the investigation and diposal by police accounted to 77.9 per cent (16,87,330 cases) of the total IPC cases for investigation during the year. These included 0.4 per cent (8877) cases where investigation was refused. The pendency requiring police disposal was 22.1 per cent in the above cases. At the end of the year, 4,79,288 cases remained pending for investigation". The report continues: "The pendency of IPC cases which awaited police disposal has been fluctuating around 20 per cent in the decade 1985-1995. However, the pendency of cases for investigation increased from 15.8 per cent in 1961 to 22 per cent in 1996. The pictorial representation of disposal of IPC cases and the increase in the magnitude of pendency during last three decades is presented below".[2]

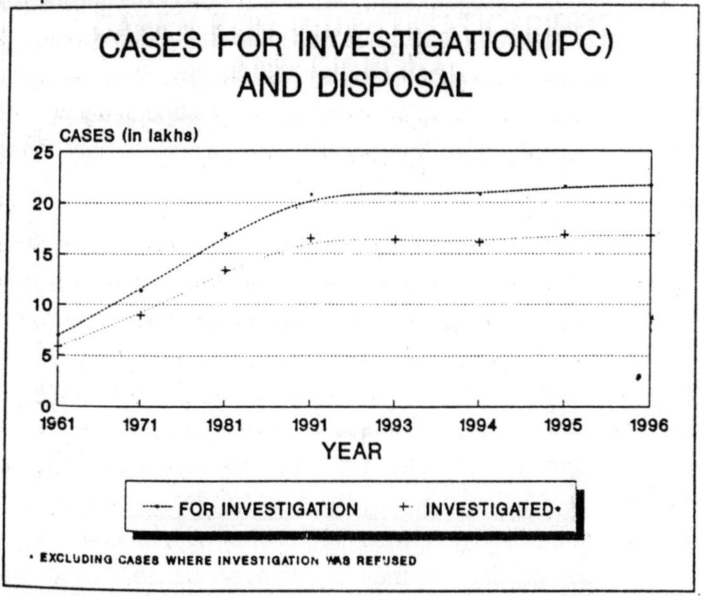

Pendency of cases is on the increase. Why? I asked some police investigators to tell me why did the pendency show an increasing trend? The answers were:

1. Investigation of crime is laborious and painstaking. Police officers may not be interested to invest their time and energy for such laborious work of patience, perseverance, persistence and perspiration. Hence, they procrastinate investigation work. I think that this sort of procrastination is an enforcement crime committed by crime investigators.

2. Criminals are educated and some of them are specialists in the commission of certain types of crime. Police investigators who lack information in advanced investigation techniques/detection methods feel diffident to investigate such cases. They put off the work and do not tell anybody about their inability or weakness in investigation work. Certainly, it is an enforcement crime.

3. Police investigators are restrained from conducting investigation in a speedier way by vested interests and interested groups which include politicians and the affluent. They, in such cases, become vulnerable to such pressures and delay the progress in investigation. This is doubtlessly an enforcement crime which just officers cannot affordx.

4. Some police officers may be very good in law and order management, but are poor in crime investigation. They lack expertise in scientific investigation and scriptory works. But, they cannot avoid investigation so long as they continue in a position. Police, as stated elsewhere, is a monopoly service and therefore one has to do all the jobs entrusted to him—no matter if one likes it or not. He may prefer the delay in investigation or approach others to offer assistance which may not be readily forthcoming or if at all available, may not be qualitatively upto the mark. In every sense, it is a dis-service done to humanity in general and to the crime doers in particular. Obviously, there is enforcement crimes in such culpable strategies.

5. Enforcement crimes in the form of employing torture, coercion, etc, come into being when police interrogation is conducted by investigators who have little professional expertise in interrogation. Investigation is a team work and many experts including professionally competent and qualitatively qualified interrogation psychologists must work together in unity. But, in India, everything including psychological interrogation is conducted by one and the same police officer whose qualifications are his uniform, police training in a general way and authority/power entrusted to him by law. Logically he abuses his power and misuses his authority and thus commits a variety of enforcement crimes.

6. People who insist immediate arrests of the suspects/crime doers are not keen in speedy investigation. This public attitude

encourages police investigators to take their own time and conduct investigation in a leisurely way. In a South Indian State, people are aggressively demanding speedy investigation in crimes against women. The National Women's Commission in a recent recommendation to Government of India has demanded time-limits for completion of investigation in crimes against women. All these show that the people are becoming increasingly aware of the undue delay in crime investigation. Some people attach many motives behind the delay in investigation.

7 Heavy workload of police investigators is another cause for delay in investigation. One and the same investigator may have to look into many cases at the same time and, more often than not, along with other police duties in jurisdiction. Bifurcation of police into two compartments, namely:(1) investigation and (2) law and order does not seem to get acceptance even now.

8. Absconding of crime doers and the inability to locate them cause further problems in crime investigation. Well informed/ educated criminals damage or destroy the evidence so intelligently and skillfully that the police are misguided, misdirected, confused or incapacitated to collect evidence that may connect the crime-doers with the crimes. What more? Identifying clues/evidence become herculian/very difficult tasks necessitating unavoidable delay in collection of evidence.

Corruption, lethargy, inaction, ignorance, disinterestedness, introductions, influences, recommendations, lack of expertise and professional skills, lack of transparency and accountability can and certainly do effect unreasonable delay in crime investigation. They too can be the causes for enforcement criminality. Many a time, multiple factors may work behind enforcement crimes.

Delay, Offences Under Special and Local Laws and Enforcement Crimes

Depending upon the types of offences and the nature of crimes, there may occur delay in crime investigation. To quote once again the report of the National Crime Records Bureau, Government of India.

"A crime head-wise analysis of pending IPC cases for police investigation reveals that the highest pendency percentage was recorded in cases of Counterfeiting' (63.4 per cent) followed by Dacoity (48.0 per cent). It is noteworthy that disposal by police of cases relating to crime against women was better than those of other offences". In some instances, delay occurs owing to factors beyond the control of the investigators. In such cases, the police cannot be blamed for enforcement crimes as they are helpless. Nevertheless, the people insist that the police are not "time conscious". And officers/men who work within the department often complain of the delay caused in disciplinary cases. Disciplinary cases can be disposed off without any delay and some cases are disposed after three or four years and there is no justification for such outright neglect of other man's hardships and mental agony in connection with facing a disciplinary inquiry".

Regarding the disposal of cases under Special and Local Laws, the NCRB report (1996) reads. "Of the total 48,34,444 cases (including the pending cases from previous year) meant for investigation, police dispose off 87.3 per cent cases including 0.5 per cent cases where investigation was denied. "The chart given below presents the figures of disposal and pendency of cases under special and local laws by police for the years 1991 to 1996".[3]

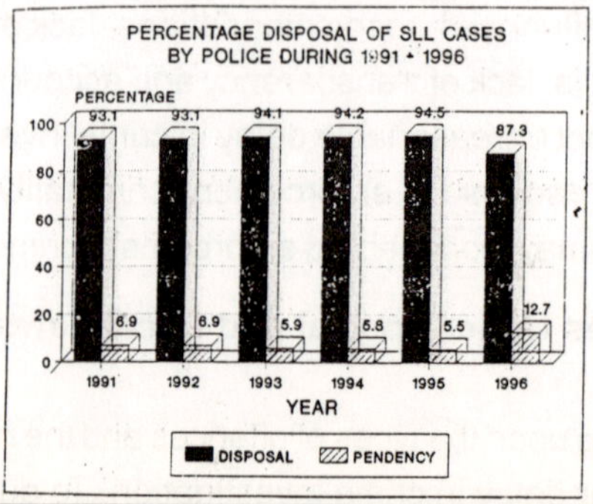

It is interesting to note that offences under certain Acts (Special and Local Laws) are not disposed off speedily. Why? Chart given below makes it clear that the pendency is less with regard to offences under Forest Act, A.C./S.T. (Prevention of Atrocities) Act, I.T.(P) Act, Prohibition Act, Gambling Act, Arms Act, etc. Pendency is more in the case of TADA Act, PCR Act, Essential Commodities Act, Anti & Art Act, etc.

PERCENTAGE DISPOSAL OF SLL CASES BY POLICE - 1996

Crime-Head	Disposal
Arms Act	82.5
NDPS Act	62.3
Gambling Act	98.1
Excise Act	74.8
Prohibition Act	84.7
Exp.&Exp.Subs.	61.1
I.T(P) Act	90.9
PCR Act	75.0
Essent. Com. Act	52.6
TADA Act	27.6
Dowry Proh.Act	68.5
SC/ST(Prev. of Atro.) Act	86.5
Ant&Art Tre Act	47.6
Forest Act	92.5

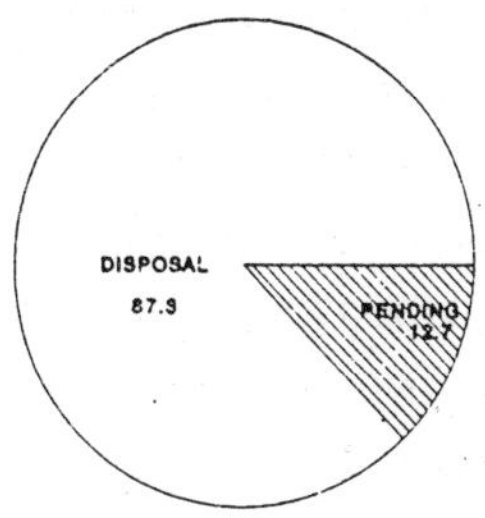

Crime-Head	Pendency
Arms Act	17.5
NDPS Act	37.7
Gambling Act	1.9
Excise Act	25.2
Prohibition Act	15.3
Exp.&Exp.Subs.	38.9
I.T.(P) Act	9.1
PCR Act	25.0
Essen. Com. Act	47.4
TADA Act	72.4
Dowry Proh. Act	31.5
SC/ST(Prev. of Atro.) Act	13.5
Ant.&Art Tre Act	52.4
Forest Act	7.5

The delay during police investigation is only the beginning of further delays subsequently. Many years are taken waiting for a judgement from the courts of law. Even petty cases charge-sheeted take 14 to 18 months for their disposal and the disposal in majority of the cases are in favour of the accused in crimes. What is the advantage of this futile exercise if prosecution ensures acquittals in majority of cases. The ordeal causes irrepairable damages to the accused, to the taxpayer and to the justice system.

Indian laws, particularly the substantial criminal laws, were framed about a century and half (1860) and the laws do not make distinction between serious offences and simple offences provided they are cognizable. Simple theft of a few rupees and a grave theft of several lakhs of rupees are treated alike and the accused in both types of offences have to undergo the same ordeal and to taste the same delay. At the end, the 'simple thief' may be punished whereas the one who commits theft of several lakhs may be acquitted. People who are accused of having commited serious offences involving multi crores of rupees become members of Parliament and participate in the deliberations in the parliament. People who have committed simple theft of a few rupees are remanded to jails as they are not granted bail. Delay in both cases are alike and what a tragedy indeed!

The antique laws enacted and enforced in India, do not have any "time-sense" and therefore the delay in investigation of cases is often condoned light-heartedly. Why think in this way? In a traffic accident case about which I have personal knowledge, the time taken for its disposal was more than four years. The case was disposed off with an acquittal verdict. There was no appeal against the same and after three and a half years, a director general of police with the help of a superintendent of police digged the buried file and the once acquitted accused was placed under suspension (The accused in the case was an officer who worked under that director general of police). The director general knew well that there was no appeal for a case which was tried long back and a judgement pronounced about four years ago. He, after placing the officer under suspension,was consulting with law department, Advocate General, Vigilance department, etc. and thus making attempts to get legal opinions. The suspended officer was reinstated in service and the case is not yet finalized even on this day (September, 1999). It is about eleven years since the issue has been under discussion for which there is yet to be any verdict. What is this? There is no accountability for anybody and the poor officer helplessly suffers the bitterness of this sort of sadist abuse of authority/power and harassment in varying degrees. This means that a few officers in the law enforcement can cause inordinate delay and persecute people. This is nothing but enforcement crime of a diabolic nature.

A situation has emerged in the country that a crime which may be punished for two or three years—even less than that—is dragged by causing inordinate delay at every stage of investigation, prosecution and trial and in certain cases, beyond the trial by appeals or by disciplinary actions. If the accused remains in the jail as a remand prisoner, he undergoes incarceration for the period. Instances are reported that prisoners remanded live in jails for seven or eight years and at the end of which the accused get judgements of honourable acquittals. And all is well that ends well-attitude is seen at the culmination. If the law is favourable to this sort of miscarriage of justice, then the law must be changed. If the human element and the human content are bad, then there is the necessity of a change in the human aspects of law enforcement—justice administration. The law enforcement functionaries are always on the prosecution side and precisely therefore they do not know the agonizing experience of the victims of inordinate delay in the so called justice administration. Should the system be so cruel to the citizens of this country? They are the people for whom the system works and they are the people who support and maintain the system—for what?—for their disadvantage? The suspect/accused is sinned against more than sinning—and this approach can never be tolerated or encouraged in any civilized country.

Registering the cases leisurely, collecting the evidence *leisurely,* investigating the cases leisurely, interrogating the suspects *leisurely,* finalizing the cases leisurely, prosecuting the case *leisurely,* conducting the trial leisurely cannot be called justice administration. The *leisurely* attitudes and approaches make defence lawyers to request for frequent adjournments on manipulated and created grounds. They cash on the weakness of the system and on the helplessness of the accused in crimes. The financial loss caused to the tax-payer and to the accused in crime may be unimaginable and the system still works on a leisure principle of administration of justice.

Notices are issued by police to witnesses, summons are sent to them, warrants are served and thus the system speedens up the procedure. But, what is the meaning of speedening mechanism if the investigation is purposefully delayed?—if the trial is purposefully delayed?—if the adjournments are frequently resorted to? 'Let the accused suffer the delay'—attitude causes more damage than advantages to many.

'Time is money and business' for many. If this is a principle applied in all areas of human transactions in a competitive world, why cannot the same principle be applied in justice administration? If the accused in a crime is innocent, then let him enjoy his freedom at an early date. If the accused is guilty, let him suffer the punishment at an early date. Delay helps to achieve neither and the impact is the suffering of sufferings and further sufferings for many years. Delay is money and business for some of the defence lawyers—and it is so for some corrupt police officers and prosecutors. Any system which allows delay without accountability and transparency allows and encourages corruption in justice administration. Allegations are there that some enforcement officials cause purposeful delay to earn money and fortune for them. Should not the law be amended fixing time limits for the completion of investigation, prosecution and trial?

The system administering justice is a mammoth agency against which the individual accused is helpless. What can the suspect/ accused in a crime do to speeden the investigation against him? To speeden the trial? He cannot do anything much except appeals, prayers, craving for mercy or humouring the agency.

Delay in the disposal of criminal cases makes the process of correction meaningless. A person who has committed a crime about 5 or 6 years ago is sentenced to imprisonment and what is the meaning of initiating corrective steps for him at that delayed time? A patient must get immediate treatment for curing the disease. Likewise, a man who commits crime must be punished at the earliest so that the correctional agencies can initiate treatment procedures at the earliest. At present, what is happening is very strange. A person who commits a crime remains in society for four or five years after the commission of his crime. After five or six years, he is punished. What type of treatment he requires then? The fact that the guilty accused is able to adjust himself without involving himself in the commission of crimes all throughout the investigation, prosecution and trial which last for several years may be a sufficient guarantee that he will adjust in society without any incarceration and correction via incarceration. Probation services today have enviable correctional value than incarceration. Many jail officers tell me that many people who come to jails on conviction do not require any correction at all. They adjust and manage themselves in prisons. Punishment thus becomes meaningless when it is awarded to guilty accused at a delayed time.

Delay and Denial of Justice

Justice delayed is justice denied—this may be a cliche-ridden expression. Everything changes in course of time. Evidence gets changed, witnesses get changed, victims of offence get changed and even the investigating officers themselves get changed. They may be subjected to many pressures and temptations and ultimately, the experience proves that delay has helped only to deny justice or further delay justice. Many investigating officers handle criminal cases when there takes place inordinate delay and different officers may have different views and opinions. Everything an investigator collects after the commission of crime cannot be transmitted to his successor in office on his transfer and precisely therefore delay means denial of justice. This is the reason why it is called an enforcement crime. "Delay the investigation"—some superior officers tell their subordinates and the intention is not to administer justice but to allow the suspects to find out means and methods to defeat the ends of justice. "Do not do things in a hurry"—the director general of police instructed his subordinate and the intention was very clear. He was asked to do so by his political bosses and it meant that all including politicians knew how to delay police investigation and thereby could defeat the objectives of crime investigator who might yield to such "orders, instructions and delay tactics". How does a police investigator delay the investigation? I asked some to narrate to me the strategies and they said: "Don't do anything to speeden investigation, but write somethings in the case-diaries so that any one who reads it will not blame you". This way of doing is also put under enforcement crime. There are several other methods. They can send something for forensic examination by the Chemical Examiner to Government and one can safely play the game if he wants to delay investigation. Just go through the case diaries in police stations and many of them are written by head-constables and station writers. The Station House Officer in some cases just endorses what the subordinates have done. Besides delaying the case, this sort of approach may misdirect the investigation in the way head-constables and station writers wish to see.

Immediately after the induction training, the sub-inspector/ assistant superintendent of police may become crime investigators. What can they do to speed up investigation unless their supervisors take due interest? As there is no law prescribing time limits for the completion of investigation (leaving apart the provisions in the code of criminal procedure prescribing limitation for certain categories of minor offences) in criminal cases, the investigating officers and their superiors are not very keen to finalize the case within a time frame. Frequent transfer of investigators and their superiors affect their interest in the matter. "What is it to me and how does it affect me if the case is delayed?"—some officers are inclined to think in this way and thus they do not want to take up cases which may displease people who are otherwise influential or powerful in society. Some cases are very complicated and painstaking. In such cases some officers are prone to think: "Why should I take up this herculian task?". Hence, they want to avoid investigation/such laborious work. This sort of approach is seen even in special units intended specially for crime investigation. Investigation of crime is less attractive for many than law and order management. To be "somebody" in territorial administration is preferred by many than to be one among many in a functional unit called crime investigation branch. Disinterestedness is another factor which affects negatively the investigation work and which causes delay in investigation. How many police officers are there known for their investigative skills and speedy detection? There may not be many. Investigative work calls for accountability and every now and then, they have to justify their acts before the courts of law. Some may not like it and as the police officers speak often: "We are handcuffed by many when we investigate crimes". If this is true, they are not very enthusiastic to be investigators and detectives in criminal cases. This sort of lack of interest and commitment make some of them to take only leisurely approach to crime investigation. Whatever that be, delay defeats justice and any attempt to delay crime investigation is an enforcement crime in every sense.

Delay : A Curse, Crime and Culture

Just recently, I addressed a group of police officers on delay in administration of justice and I said that the delay had become a curse, a culture and a crime in India. Whether or not it is due to rule of law or lack of accountability or irresponsible and utter unconcern towards the victims of delay or whatever, it must be treated as a crime, heinous crime in every sense. I wrote a series of articles in a Malayalam daily *Madhyamam* and got them published about a few years ago. Some lawyers in the High Court of, Kerala met me when I went there to address the Bar Association and told me that delay was the cause of miscarriage of justice. Yet, delay could be seen everywhere and in a culture which tolerates delay, anything done in speed is treated as a crime or charity done in a special way to a favourite individual. In my book on *Crime and Society: Current Issues and Trends,* the Problem of Hoarding of Files has been discussed and an idea that hoarding of files in the existing administrative culture must be treated as a crime. Red tapism and administrative delay, etc, are sweet words which are laughed at by the bureaucracy and there is no effective means initiated till now to solve the problem. So long as time limits are not fixed for the disposal of files, it is certain that the malady will continue to be ramified and percolated down.

Delay in administration of justice, if treated as an enforcement crime, can ensure that the ends of criminal justice is achieved. Otherwise, the conviction rate is likely to go up to an extent that the entire exercise may become an exercise in futility—an exercise without any purpose being served—a ritual that warrants a lot of money from the public exchequer and in reality a waste of money, manpower and resources. The present system which permits delay in administration of justice makes people dissatisfied and is a cause for the loss of public trust and confidence of people on the system. A situation has now emerged in which the accused in crimes make press conferences demanding punishment for the crimes they have committed. A few years ago, the papers brought out such a demand from some people whose cases were pending for decision for more than ten years. Indecision and prolonged uncertainty in criminal cases make all unhappy and disturbed.

There was a time when retributive theory of criminal justice was in vogue. Ultimately, what the society achieved were law made cripples who became more a liability to society than advantage. Almost in a similar way, the hung suspects/accused in crimes—who wait for a decision in the alleged crimes—become a liability for the society.

An accused in a crime remains as an accused until the case is disposed off and he finds it extremely difficult to get a job and impossible to leave the locality. He is either bailed out or remanded to jail custody. In both cases, he is looked down upon and remains as a burden to society. If human happiness and social welfare are what may be desired for by administration of just justice, then the disposal of criminal cases must take place in a speedier way within a time frame. The unwillingness to move things in the right direction is resented at by many and reacted adversely by human rights activists and well meaning citizens. Go to a police station, to a prison for remanding undertrials, to a court of law, you may hear the cries of several people praying for speedy disposal of cases registered against them. The delay punishes not only the suspects/accused but also his family and kith and kin. This indeed is an injustice done to humanity.

Delay and Justification

One who causes delay can find out any amount/number of justifications, rationalizations and explanations for the delay. For, he is not the sufferer in the case. Investigation, prosecution and trial—all of them are routine matters for that privileged group entrusted with job. Hence, any delay may not affect them. After some time, the personnel responsible for the delay may be transferred out and his duty is to entrust the delayed cases to his successor in office. In extreme cases only, disciplinary actions are initiated for the delay caused in criminal cases.

Lack of adequate number of investigating officers, lack of facilities, lack of assistance, lack of encouragement, lack of supervision, lack of... lack of ...., lack of many things may cause delay in investigation and all these "lacks" cannot be a solution to the sufferer of these "lacks". The wearer alone knows where the shoe pinches and many who stand around him cannot and do not know the agony and sleeplessness which the sufferer bitterly suffers. The society has entrusted the work to the responsible concern and care of the law enforcement agencies and if delay takes place, it means an utter unconcern to people's expectations and aspirations. A crisis between expectations and obligations take place and the crisis may lead to the collapse of the system.

Police Commissions, Law Commissions, judges, legislators, police officers, and so on, know the pathetic situation, but they are more inclined to think from their point of view and so far the delay in administration of justice could not be reduced. There are exhortations, public utterances, sermons, circulars, etc. coming from various quarters, but the people at the receiving end do not feel the difference. They continue to tolerate the delay and often complain that the issue is not evaluated from the sufferer's point of view. Proposals are pending with the Governments to bifurcate the police into two:(i) Crime Investigation, (ii) Law and Order—so that the crime investigation unit can give full time attention to crime investigation. But, such proposals are not attended to with seriousness. Proposals are also there for the establishment of more criminal courts in proportion to the increase in criminal cases and police investigators. They too are under perpetual consideration and deep study by the decision making authorities.

People talk a lot about administration of justice, but do very little to administer just justice. Why? Many still entertain the retributive and deterrent attitude and approaches to crime doers and victims of enforcement criminality. Research and development is lacking in the area and therefore there takes place very little improvement in this area. The antique laws and ancient procedures which existed in an era of bullock carts cannot do justice in an era of computers and sattellites. The laws must be changed making delay as an enforcement crime and hoarding of files as an offence under the penal laws. Justice is for the people and if the existing legislations can not cater to the needs of the hour, they must be buried along with old concepts of justice administration. Third millenium represents accountability and transparency in justice administration and any delay that lacks accountability and transparency must be treated with penal sanction. Justice must be done and it must be done at the best time. Delay defeats both and to reiterate a cliche: 'justice delayed is justice denied'.

References

1. *Crime in India—1996,* National Crime Records Bureau, Government of India, 1998.
2. *Crime in India—1996, ibid.*
3. *Crime in India—1996, ibid.*

6
DISCIPLINARY JUSTICE

Recently, I met a retired director general of police at a marriage function. He asked me: "How are you?". I did not answer his question. Instead I asked him: "How are you, Sir?". Then he told me: "I think that I am outliving my utility". It was a shocking reply indeed. Why? Why did he think so? I told him: "Sir, heaven's sake, don't think so. If you start thinking so, then life becomes meaningless". He just smiled and said: "I feel that I am being rejected by people whom I have helped in many ways in service". I could understand the agony of a director general of police who occupied such a high position in bureaucracy now that he was out of his office. However, I asked some police officers "why did he feel so"? Then came the responses that:

1. He was one who had a punitive mind/punishing mentality in disciplinary cases.

2. He has never reduced the punishment when he reviewed or heard appeals. People were afraid to make appeals in disciplinary proceedings as they knew that the penalty would only be enhanced.

One's concept about discipline, disciplinary justice, disciplinary proceedings and discipline-administration may vary and in some instances, it may be against the principles of natural justice. The result will be enforcement crimes.

On the personal level, I had a bitter experience. I did help an officer in many ways, but when he became my superior by virtue of his office, he initiated steps against me and got an order from the Government to conduct an inquiry against me. The motivating forces for such an action are yet unknown to me. Whatever that be, people who occupy higher positions seem to forget their past and are found to be prone to cause considerable difficulties to the subordinates. At the end of the harassments, the officer under inquiry may be exonerated and as it is today, there is no provision in law to get victimological compensation to the suffered. The officers/men who face disciplinary inquiries thus become victims of abuse of power/authority by the disciplinary authority.

One day I found a superintendent of police shedding tears in his office. I asked him: "What is the matter?" He told me: "I have not done anything good to him—anything bad to him. Yet, he initiated disciplinary action against me". Why do people think in this way? There is a view that the etiology of initiating disciplinary actions against another can be anything from a bad motive to a good motive. No noteworthy research studies have been done in this area to find out the causative aspects of enforcement crimes in disciplinary matters. However, how many disciplinary cases end in punishment? The percentage is not very high. How many punished personnel approach Administrative Tribunals? They too are a few.

How many disciplinary cases are judged to be irregular, unnecessary or against the principles of natural justice? No studies have been conducted so far on them. Nevertheless, a casual look into the decisions pronounced by the courts may show that many cases are judged in favour of the punished.

It is roughly estimated that 10 per cent of the lower and middle level functionaries in police may be under a disciplinary inquiry at any given time. If that is true, then there is something wrong in the discipline of the so called disciplinary service.

Causes of Disciplinary Inquiries and Enforcement Crimes

I had many occasions to discuss with police officers/men about the causes of disciplinary actions against them. If their versions are true, then the causes of disciplinary enquiries may be:

1. Ego clashes between subordinate and superiors and interpersonnel rivalry.
2. Hostility, vengeance, vindictiveness of the higher ups towards the lower ranks.
3. Pervert concepts about discipline and disciplinary offences.
4. Insistance of 'parade ground discipline' in interpersonal relations in other areas in police work and subsequent interpretation of behaviour which may be justified otherwise.
5. Prejudices, bias, preconceived notions against subordinates.
6. Exercise of pseudo-authority or abuse of authority.
7. Lack of understanding about disciplinary justice and the punitive mind among the disciplinary authorities.
8. Desire to exercise one's authority on subordinates under a deterrent umbrella.
9. Genuine grounds for which disciplinary actions are the only option.
10. Pressure from extra-departmental sources to initiate disciplinary actions against officers/men pointed out by them.
11. Pressure from departmental higher ups to whom the disciplinary authority is subordinate.
12. Political influence and pressure exerted by the affluent and the influential.
13. Court orders or observations by courts of law or commissions of inquiry.
14. Recommendations by the authority which conducts preliminary inquiry and establishment of a *prima facie* ground for initiating further action.

15. Desire and determination to cause harassment and sleeplessness to the subordinates.

Thus, one may see that a disciplinary inquiry may originate on many grounds and it depends much upon how the disciplinary authority looks at it. There is a school of thought that only 30-35 percent of the disciplinary inquiries are justified and the rest can be managed without disciplinary inquiries being initiated and conducted. Disciplinary inquiry is only one method to correct an erring official and management experts may subscribe to the view that disciplinary inquiries are less effective to correct a person than other strategies which may be more effective to establish disciplinary justice.

Any disciplinary inquiry which is not justifiable is an enforcement crime of misuse of power an abuse of authority. In disciplinary inquiries, the crime is not committed individually by the disciplinary authority. Researches show that there is co-operation among various ranks in doing the evil against the 'so called' delinquent. In the case of a superior authority insisting a lower authority to it to initiate disciplinary action against someone, one sees intrinsically unjust act and it is certainly a crime. It is never licit to obey such unlawful orders. I have seen some inquiring officers (in disciplinary inquiries) complaining that they are doing an unjust act. Being people having a morally upright conscience, they find it extremely difficult to co-operate with the evil intention of unscrupulous authorities who initiate disciplinary inquiries. Nevertheless they do them, for, they want to survive in the department—otherwise, they may have to sacrifice their prestigious positions in the department or to relinquish their reasonable hope for career advancement. Hence, the disciplinary authorities and the inquiry authorities—even if they can misuse their power/authority—are under grave obligation of conscience not to commit enforcement crimes in the name of discipline or in the pretext of administering disciplinary justice. It is never licit to co-operate in evils. Their co-operation can never be justified either by invoking respect for the position they hold or for the larger interest of disciplinary justice.

An official write-up by the police department in a South Indian State reads : "The police force requires a very high standard of discipline. The work connected with disciplinary proceedings occupies an important place in the functions of supervision. The morale of the service can be kept up only if offenders against discipline are suitably punished". The critics on this say that the words "morale", "offences" and "discipline" in police need further clarifications and clarity. Offences are not well clarified in any rules, discipline is not well clarified and morale is not well understood. The concepts have undergone changes in the democracy and the disciplinary authority must become sensitive to the changing and the changed meanings of the words "offence, discipline and morale". Punishment and disciplinary actions may be methods of enforcing discipline. But, there are other methods which are more powerful than the punitive steps.

Enforcement Crimes During Disciplinary Inquiries

Among enforcement crimes, suspension comes first. According to Oxford Dictionary, suspension means "temporary deprivation of one's office or position". But, in reality it is much more than that and the disciplinary authority knows it. In some instances, suspension is ordered as a mode of punishment although the case law is that it is not a punishment. A circle inspector of police was once suspended. A preliminary inquiry was initiated. He was kept under suspension for eight months. Preliminary inquiry revealed no *prima facie* ground for initiating disciplinary inquiry against him. He was reinstated to service. He suffered a lot owing to his suspension and social humiliation. What name, other than enforcement crime, can be given to such misuse of authority and abuse of power? See some of the judgements from the courts of law.

1. Rule does not empower retrospective suspension.[1]
2. Recourse to suspension may not be deemed as a matter of routine pointing out to reckless and cavalier exercise of

power without the necessary circumspection and adequate application of mind[2].

3. Suspension with retrospective effect is illegal[3].

4. Although suspension is not a punishment, an order of suspension is not to be lightly passed against the Government servant. It results in grave civil consequences to the officer[4].

There is no accurate estimate of the number of police personnel placed under suspension in police department. Among the middle level functionaries, there are many who had suffered the bitterness of suspenion and I interviewed a few of them. They stated that:

1. The cause of suspension was political pressure.
2. The cause of suspension was media coverage.
3. The cause of suspension was ill will of the superior ranks.
4. The cause of suspension was vindictiveness--ego-clashes—enimity—harassment—humilation, etc, and thus it may be seen that many grounds which form the causes of suspension may not be the causes at all even if they are seen in departments other than police. It may be further seen that the causes which make grounds of suspension for the lower level functionaries may not become grounds at all for higher levels. In some States in India, Special Police, Discipline, Inquiries, Punishments and Appeal Rules are enacted to initiate disciplinary inquiries against lower and State level officers whereas the same are not seen at top levels. They are dealt by the rules applicable to all other civil servants. Why? The double standard in approach in disciplinary justice may work as a source of committing enforcement crimes. The laws and rules en trust subordinates' career and future to the responsible concern and care of the disciplinary authority and superiors,

not at all to make arbitary use of them, but to maintain them with wisdom and to administer justice for them with justness and fidelity. But, are the superiors and authority aware of their responsibility?

Victims of suspension make complaints that the enthusiasm/ overenthusiasm to see that somebody is placed under suspension is not shown in an equal measure/in a minimum measure to see that the suspended is given subsistence allowance or the suspension order is reviewed at the proper time stipulated by the rules or reminded by an upright conscience. The subsistence allowance is also called "suspension allowance" and in all sense, the allowance has a suspension taste also. Owing to delayed review of suspension or payment of subsistence allowance, some employees suffer in many ways under several counts. This sort of victimization is certainly an enforcement crime and the authority responsible must be made accountable for the culpable responsibility and callous indifference which he expresses. A deputy superintendent of police was placed under suspension for showing misbehaviour in public. A petty case was registered against him and the case was honourably acquitted. He was placed under suspension and even after 15 months he was not reinstated.Why? He was not even issued with a memo of charges and the injustice was perpetuated without any prick of conscience. Is it not an enforcement crime to do so? It is an administrative crime intrinsically incompatible with human dignity, yet it is being committed with immunity from criminal liability for the acts and accountability for what they do. The top level administration knows it, but it refuses to interfere in it. What is the loss caused to public exchequer by this sort of inaction, lethargy, willful negligence and injustice? When the inquiry is over, the delinquent may be reinstated in service (if he is exonerated) and the Government gives him everything causing heavy financial loss to the public revenue. The negative attitudes and approaches in administration of disciplinary justice make it clear that the choice of certain ways of acting which may be radically incompatible with the dignity of people are tolerated or appreciated in government administration.

Enforcement Crimes and Conduct of Inquiries

How many officers in police know the correct procedure in the conduct of inquiries? Many, to be honest, do not know the exact meaning of the word *"Quasi-judicial"* in disciplinary inquiries. Principles of natural justice applicable to disciplinary inquiries are unknown to some. I have seen that some police officers who work in the armed batallions/reserve are finding it extremely difficult to conduct inquiries in a quasi-judicial way. They depend upon their writer constables/ head constables/civilian staff to do the same. They cannot be blamed for their ignorance as they are not exposed to any sort of training in the subject. By virtue of their position or designation, such people get opportunities to conduct disciplinary inquiries with little or no knowledge about the procedure. Some who are promoted from the rank of constable—who are not educated well—too conduct disciplinary inquiries. What will be the end of such inquiries? Surely, they will pave the way to commit enforcement crimes. The lower and the lowest level functionaries who are at the receiving end become the victims of such miscarriage of justice in disciplinary cases.

Preliminary enquiry has some purpose. The officer/man against whom preliminary enquiry is conducted can waive his right to give an explanation—can refuse to participate in the enquiry—can show non-co-operation and he need not know that such an enquiry is conducted against him. These being the case-laws well settled in disciplinary cases, some officers pressure the officer/man under enquiry to speak out many things—threaten him—coerces him and sometimes gives false promises that his interest will be looked after. Some unscrupulous inquiry officers meet the disciplinary authority to know his intention and write the reports accordingly. They make the witnesses to give statements in the way they want—either strengthening the case or weakening the case under enquiry. Disciplinary enquiry is conducted to find out the truth and if this is the way an inquiry is conducted, what good can come from such an inquiry?

Doubtlessly, the end result will be enforcement crimes.

Every enquiry—preliminary and formal (regular)—is and should be the affirmation of an inseparable connection between the authority and a subordinate and it should not be contaminated by unjust procedures and strategies. Not only must disciplinary justice be administered, but it must be protected with responsible concern towards the officer/man under inquiry. The meaning of disciplinary justice is found in ensuring justness and in this context, human conscience must have true and full significance. Such an administration of justice alone ensures the morale, discipline, service and confidence among the members of police department.

In one case, an officer in police department was placed under suspension after eight years after the incident took place. There were four court judgements in favour of the officer under inquiry. There was no adverse observation of the court against him. The director general of police who had an axe to grind with the officer wrote a special report to the Government misrepresenting facts and saw to it that the officer was placed under suspension. Preliminary enquiry and the principles in the conduct of inquiries had no meaning for him who had no respect for human dignity. Honestly, many felt relieved when that director general retired from service. When a person is elevated to the position of the director general of police, he must show profound honour to justice administration and in the above case, he committed a serious enforcement crime. On further study about his past life in service, it was learnt that he was not rated to be a justice friendly police officer throughout his career. In some cases, preliminary enquiry is conducted and in some other cases an enquiry by the Special Branch, CID is conducted. In other cases, no preliminary enquiry is conducted. Yet in other cases, a preliminary enquiry by a favourite officer is conducted and thus it may be noticed that there is no uniformity in approaches and procedures. Subjective scales are applied in some and in all cases, invariably some hardship is caused. This approach and procedure has caused distrust among the subordinate ranks, so much so, that the ends of disciplinary justice are defeated. Of course, the courts of law have ruled that preliminary enquiry is not essential to initiate disciplinary action against an employee. This is applicable more in private sectors. Government being a public organization, it is always advisable to have a preliminary enquiry being conducted in an objective way to establish a *prima facie* case against the officer under enquiry. Ignorance of the rules alone is not the cause of miscarriage of justice, rather is the perverted attitude that the authority has. Where the life and career may be involved, the service of justness must be profoundly consistent. Allegations are heard that some disciplinary authorities create disciplinary enquiries just to overlook somebody who is in disfavour with them. Justness in disciplinary matters cannot tolerate bias, and discrimination, for one's career and future are of paramount importance at every stage and in every situation. The disciplinary authority must show care and concern for all who work under him. Indeed, at an even deeper level, the authority needs to go to the very roots of one's life and career before he arbitrarily decides to initiate disciplinary proceedings against a subordinate. The subordinate at the receiving end at times is a helpess person who may be condemned to knock at the door of mercy shown by the disciplinary auhtority who initiates action against him.

Formal Inquiry and Enforcement Crimes

An inquiry officer is appointed and he functions as a quasi-judicial authority, sometimes without knowing the ABC of natural justice. What is the eligibility and suitability of the inquiring officers in police? Designation or the position one holds in the department alone is the eligibility. The suitability is fixed on the basis of nothing or his favourable disposition towards the disciplinary authority. The judgements from the courts of law may reveal that the inquiring officers are people who need information on the conduct of formal inquiries:

* The enquiry officer took into consideration his personal knowledge about the petitioner while deciding as to whether the pe-

titioner was guilty of the charges levelled against him. The punishment imposed was illegal[5].

* The act of the presiding officer in having his own testimony recorded in the case indubitably evidences a state of mind which clearly discloses considerable bias against the delinquent. It is against all canons of fair play[6].

* Cross examination of defence witnesses by the enquiry officer was in plain violation of the principles of natural justice and consequently the inquiry proceedings were vitiated[7].

One may thus find thousands of judgements showing the ineligibility and unsuitability of inquiry officers in disciplinary proceedings. In one case, I found the inquiry officer who was an additional director general of police contacting his colleagues over telephone and depending upon the office superintendent to clarify his doubts when the formal inquiry session was in progress. The officer under inquiry objected to the procedure, but in vain, was threatened to keep quite. The same inquiry officer got in touch with the disciplinary authority—in front of the officer under inquiry—to give instructions as to what to do and how to go about during the progress of formal inquiry. I thought pity and asked to myself: "What sort of inquiry is this?". This is enforcement crime and precisely, therefore, cannot be tolerated. What does it profit if an enquiry officer says that he has the eligibility and suitability to conduct formal inquiry, but does it in an unjust way? The results may be appeals, review petitions and court cases. How many lower level functionaries will be able to or be prepared to undergo the ordeals connected with such disciplinary enquiries? Why can't disciplinary tribunals be established for the purpose? It is a pressing need at the present time when the subordinates feel that there is a "culture of disciplinary injustice" which forcefully opposes a "culture of justice" in police department. More than that, it is a need which is required to establish trust in disciplinary authorities. If a subordinate is ill-clad and in lack of trust on disciplinary proceedings and the disciplinary authority tells him "I administer justice", without giving him the psychological satisfaction that justice has been administered, what does it profit? So disciplinary justice by itself, if it has no worth, is dead. In the conduct of an inquiry, the authority must be inspired and distinguished by specific attitude, knowledge and justness: he must care for the officer under inquiry as a person for whom the law has made him responsible.

I have observed that some inquiry officers are reluctant or refuse to record the statements of witnesses during the inquiry. They allow an office superintendent/writer constable to do the work. They think that it is below their dignity to do so. Whatever that be, some of them do not conduct the inquiry keeping in view the disciplinary jurisprudence. I have seen an inquiry officer asking questions to the witnesses and he allowed the officer under inquiry to cross-examine the witnesses immediately after each question was asked. His ignorance about the procedure to examine and cross-examine witnesses was not corrected even when it was pointed out that the procedure was wrong. The reason for his refusal to be corrected was that the assistant who aided him did not allow him to conduct the inquiry in the correct way. Courts have ruled that the inquiry authority is not deemed to delegate his authority to an assistant during the inquiry. The rules were also very clear and specific, yet he allowed an assistant to record everything during the inquiry.

Whenever an inquiry is conducted in a manner not satisfying the officer/man under inquiry, it ceases to have any impact on establishing discipline. A haphazard inquiry causes indiscipline in the department. There is undue delay in completion of inquiry and the consequence is that the officer/man under inquiry suffers the sufferings. How long can an inquiry continue? There is no specific rule specifying limitations and as a result, some inquiries last for several years. An inquiry was initiated on 18 April, 1995 and it is not over even on 28 August, 1999. In another case an officer was placed under suspension and the inquiry commenced after 10 months. It continued for an unreasonably long time and ultimately, he approached the High Court to get a directive to complete the inquiry within a reasonable time. The court ordered that the inquiry ought to be completed within three months. The disciplinary authority prayed for more time and the Court allowed another three months. The inquiry was over and the order regularizing the suspension period was not issued for five long years. Why? There was no satisfactory explanation for it. The authorities said: "He has gone to Court. Let him go to court for getting another order prescribing time for the issuing of the regularization order". The authority knew that going to a court was expensive and the intention was the denial of annual increments and it seemed that the persecution gave the authority a sort of pleasure. Is it not an enforcement crime to do so? If it is not an enforcement crime, then what is it? The disciplinary authority, as a rule, is not concerned about such things and the impact is dissatisfaction and displeasure within the department. Thus, the life of the individuals in the department is persecuted by conditions of hardship, maladjustment, mental tension and rejection. Is this discipline in the department? Whenever disciplinary authority denies or neglects its fundamental duty, the subordinates think that the authority is its own rule and measure. Such an authority has no justification to demand discipline within the organization. Purposeful delay in finalizing disciplinary proceedings is an objectionable act and very much an enforcement crime. The victims of such willful commission of enforcement crimes must be entitled to get victimological compensation from the authority responsible for the same. To cause delay or to assist delay in disciplinary inquiries is a crime against humanity/individual officers and men under inquiry. Responsibility for it falls on superior officers. No rule or law accepts deliberate delaying of decisions by superior officers/disciplinary authority under any circumstances. Delay in completing disciplinary inquiry must be treated as a grave misconduct for initiating disciplinary action against those who delay the proceedings.

De Novo Inquiries and Enforcement Crimes

Sometimes the disciplinary authority writes: "Conduct a *de novo* inquiry". What does it mean? It means nothing but further delaying the process. How many times an authority may write De novo inquiry?—until such time he receives a report that satisfies him? An IAS Officer of 25 years of administrative experience wrote, while he was holding the charge of the Secretary (Home), to conduct a *de novo*inquiry. He was pointed out the well settled law that there was no *de novo* inquiry in disciplinary justice. He could not be satisfied. He said: "Don't come here to teach me". His IAS ego could not tolerate the cry of an officer under inquiry. The ruling is that the "disciplinary authority cannot order a *de novo* enquiry. Where the findings of the enquiring authority are adverse to the delinquent officer, it is open to the disciplinary authority to consider the material and evidence, come to a different conclusion and exonerate him from charges. If on the other hand, the enquiry authority holds that the charges are not proved, it is open to the disciplinary authority to take a different view and record findings. Where the disciplinary authority is satisfied that some evidence which would have been available was not collected by the inquiring authority, it may even direct the enquiring authority to proceed further with order a *de novo* enquiry after wiping out the enquiry already conducted".[8]

In another landmark judgement, the court observed: "There is no provision in the rule for completely setting aside previous enquiries on the ground that the reports of inquiring officer or officers do not appeal to disciplinary authority".[9] Initiate an inquiry, entrust it to an ignorant inquiry officer, conduct it in a manner which is against the principles of natural justice, cause purposeful delay to reinstate a suspended employee, delayed review in suspended cases, non—payment of subsistence allowance in time, preparation of report and ordering for *de novo* inquiry—and thus the enforcement crimes committed by the so called "disciplinary authority" are numerous. There is no effective remedy for the atrocities committed in the name of administering disciplinary justice or in the pretext of administering disciplinary justice.

In India, the disciplinary authority, as the living image of justice, is entrusted by the law and people in a democracy to exercise power and authority. The authority, if it does not exercise its power with dignity, it means that enforcement crimes will dominate the administration. People who have administrative dominion over other lesser mortals in the department when cause miscarriage of justice, behave not for the dignity of the department but for his selfish interest.

No enquiry was conducted even after the lapse of two and a half years after the occurrence and it was held by the court that no fair and effective inquiry could be conducted unless it commenced within a reasonable time after the incident. To call upon an employee to defend himself at this distance of time is probably to put him at considerable disadvantage and thus deny him the benefit of natural justice—said the Court.[10] Once I cited the above judgement in a class and thereafter I got at least two dozen calls from police for knowing more about the contents of the judgement. I asked them: "Why do you want the full text of the judgement?" and they said that they were facing disciplinary inquiries on things that happened about six, seven, eight years ago. All of them narrated stories about the onset or initiation of inquiries at such a delayed time. Behind every case, I could see some ego clashes, personality fights, previous enemity, hostility or vindictiveness, etc. I could not find any justifiable reason in most of the cases for taking up a forgotten incident by digging up the files which were buried long back.

To harass or victimize a subordinate in the name of justice is a serious crime. At every level of police administration, one may see tragic cases of disciplinary inquiries. The authority to administer justice to the subordinates must never be misused to harm them. If one does so, the intrinsic values in human life become meaningless in disciplinary justice. People entrusted to protect their subordinates must desist from causing harm to others. I could see right in front of my eyes some "authorities" who exercised their powers aggressively against their fellow brethren when they were in police service becoming "things" to be avoided when they have retired from service. Authorities who treated their subordinates with utter disregard and without showing any respect for human dignity have become mere "things" for human hatred and avoidance. Authorities, while they punish people, should offer an incentive and help to change their behaviour. If human treatment and corrective steps are sufficient to change one's behaviour, then the disciplinary authority must limit itself to such steps, for such actions are more in conformity to the dignity of human person in administrative justice. In the case of Bani Singh, an officer of the Indian Police Service, disciplinary proceedings were initiated after 12 years after the incident had taken place. He approached Central Administrative Tribunal and the order was quashed. The State went for an appeal and the Supreme Court while disposing the appeal stated that the inordinate delay in initiating action could not be justified. Nobody knew the amount of money, the appellant had to spend to get an order from the Supreme Court and for the disciplinary authority, it was only a routine matter and there was enough public fund for the purpose. In police department, there exist ample opportunities for the superiors to initiate disciplinary actions against any one. Police have associations, but their strength is weak and voice is feeble if they see administrative injustice. Nevertheless, the trend is getting changed in the recent past, so much so, that police associations, particularly of the constabulary react to administrative injustice in disciplinary cases in a selective way. The trend is likely to be strengthened in the years to come. Sometimes, the IPS associations too voice against unjustified departmental actions against their fellow colleagues in the IPS fraternity.

Punishments and Enforcement Crimes

There are two types of punishments—major and minor. To what type of misconducts, the minor punishment should be awarded? OR the major punishment must be given? There are no specific guidelines for it. It depends fully and totally on the discretion of the disciplinary authority—rather on the whims and fancies of the punishing authority.

For the same misconduct, one may be issued with a charge-sheet for minor penalty and another may be given a charge-sheet for a major penalty. It is as good as telling that a murderer can be punished with fine or with death penalty at the sweet desire of the disciplinary authority. In other words, one may be punished by awarding a censure and another by an order of dismissal. What are scales to decide the punishment? The only scale is the subjective decision of the disciplinary authority. Once a police vehicle was misused by a senior officer, then he was issued with a charge-sheet for minor penalty. In another case, a police vehicle was misused by a head constable. He was issued with a major penalty charge-sheet and finally he was dismissed from service. The Servant's Conduct rules speak about misconducts, but do not specify punishment for each of the misconducts. This sort of arbitrary decisions in determining punishments may be a cruel source of injustice and fertile field to commit enforcement crimes.

Disciplinary authority is expected to administer justice objectively and its sense of fair justice must far exceed the dimensions of its partiality, favouritism, narrow-mindedness, perverted views about justice administration, vindictiveness, hostility, etc., because it consists in sharing the very aspirations of the people who have appointed him to exercise the role of a disciplinary authority in departmental inquiries. The loftiness of this divine authority to punish people must reveal the greatness and the inestimable value of justice administration in disciplinary matters.

Many of the misconducts shown in the Conduct Rules which were enacted decades ago are not misconducts now. But, in the hands of an unscrupulous authority everything becomes a misconduct. He may exercise his powers not for the greater good of department or people, but for the greater glory of his ego-projections and authority. Some of the judgements pronounced by the courts on the enforcement crimes committed by the so named punishing authorities may reveal that few of them lack any sense of justice. I, for one, think that most unfortunately, this disturbing state of affairs far from decreasing, is expanding. Certainly, the trend is an attack on the dignity of human beings.

* The penalty imposed must commensurate with the gravity of the misconduct. Any penalty disproportionate to the gravity of the misconduct would be violative of Article 14 of the Constitution.[11]

* Merely the use of indiscret, indecent or threatening language to a superior officer on one occasion unconnected with any subsequent positive action and not preceded by any blame-worthy conduct during the long years of service can not permit an extreme penalty of dismissal from service.[12]

* Imposition of two penalties—one of censure and another of recovery of loss on the delinquent is illegal[13].

There is an allegation that the provisions in Discipline, Inquiries, Punishments and Appeal Rules are misused by authorities with punitive mind. "An employee convicted in a criminal case was given the benefit under Section 4 (1) of the Probation of Offenders Act, 1958. On the ground that he was convicted, the department imposed on him a penalty of stoppage of three increments with cumulative effect without conducting any enquiry or affording any opportunity. The order was held to be illegal by the court.[14]

In another case, *Muraleedharan Nair V. State of Kerala*[15], police department removed the circle inspector on the ground that he was convicted by a court in a criminal case. Kerala High Court held the view that "conviction by a criminal court will not automatically entitle dismissal or removal of the civil servant from service. Muraleedharan Nair had 16 years of service in police department and during this period, he was awarded a large number of merit certificates, cash awards and good service entries in the service records. Taking into consideration of his merit and ability, he was promoted to the post of circle inspector of police in the year 1994.

He had an unblemished service career". The Court observed that the retention of Muraleedharan Nair in service can by no stretch of imagination be constructed as one against the interest of public service. The court ordered reinstatement of the circle inspector forthwith.

What does it mean? The people in authority take arbitrary, illegal and pain-causing decisions which are violative of all canons of law in disciplinary cases. The merits, efficiency and ability of the officer are not taken into account. The totality of a person and his personality are not given any consideration in some cases. Why? Whatever is opposed to administration of disciplinary justice—whatever violates the principles of natural justice—whatever insults human dignity all these things and others like them are infamou indeed. They poison the disciplinary atmosphere in the department and they do more harm to those who practice them in the name of administering justice in departmental inquiries than those who suffer the injury. Moreover, they are a supreme dishonour to the ends of disciplinary justice in a democracy.

How are the penalties imposed? In some cases, proceedings for imposition of major penalty may be initiated. Later, the inquiry may be conducted by following minor penalty procedure. And what is the criterion for such a shift? No criterion, but the desire of the authority works here. In *Raveendranathan V.District Collector,* the Court observed: "After having initiated disciplinary proceedings for imposition of a major penalty, the disciplinary authority cannot make a short cut by choosing to impose a minor penalty, without properly completing the enquiry following the procedure prescribed in that behalf.[16]

The authority stands at a higher pedestal than the officer under inquiry. Precisely therefore, the authority is in an advantageous position. There are many cases in which the appellate authority has altered minor penalties to major penalties. This is done, sometimes, even without issuing any notice to the employee and without hearing him. This is illegal.[17] But, how to establish the illegality?—through a second appeal?—through a revision or review?—through a court order? All these are expensive, time consuming laborious and painstaking efforts. Does a lower level employee have money to fight against these sorts of crimes? If he does not have, then let him suffer the consequences. What else can he do? It is roughly estimated that nearly 10 per cent of the convicts in many prisons are innocent people. It can also be stated that a fixed percentage of the punished in disciplinary inquiries too may be innocent people. Sometimes, the punished people are overlooked in promotions. The Supreme Court in *B.C. Chaturvedi V.Union of India* has clearly laid down that "there is no rule saying that a person against whom a disciplinary proceeding is pending should not be promoted at all. There is no illegality if promotion is ordered subject to the decision in disciplinary proceedings.[18]

Disciplinary Inquiry, Public Interest and Enforcement Crimes

How much money is simply wasted for conducting departmental inquiries? No study has been conducted in this area. Yet, it will be several lakhs/crores. In how many inquiries, the officers/men under inquiry are exonerated ? What is the loss to public exchequer in such cases? What is the public interest in wasting money, time and manpower in the name of administration of disciplinary justice? There are countries where the authority who initiates disciplinary enquiries is punished in cases the officer/man under inquiry is exonerated. There are countries in which exonerated employees are paid remuneration/victimological compensation for the sufferings they undergo during the process and progress of inquiries. In such countries, studies show that disciplinary inquiries are conducted only in genuine cases and that too with convincing evidence. An authority, however supreme it is, should not be allowed to misuse its powers or abuse its authority in the pretext of administering justice. In India, at present, there exists no law/rule for paying victimological compensation in disciplinary cases. As a result, the higher ups may cause terror and exploit the weakness of the lower level employees in the name of disciplinary justice. The disciplinary authority does many things with immunity or without any accountability.

Just go through the provisions contained in Government Servants' Conduct Rules. One may find then that the entire rules are framed to see that there exists a master-servant relationship. In private sectors, 'some one' who has invested money is there and the employees are accountable to him. In Government service, who is the owner? The owner may be the people and as such there is a saying that the government's business is everybody's business which is nobody's business. As such, no one as an individual is ever a disciplinary authority and as such the master-servant relationship between superiors and subordinates at a given time is temporary. People come and people go as authorities, superiors or subordinates as the case may be. One may initiate an inquiry and another may drop it. Some may show greater enthusiasm to conduct an inquiry in a quick way and another may purposefully delay it. It so happens that the inquiring authority is often appointed by designation and more often than not the inquiry officers are transferred out often, so much so, there may be three or four enquiry officers for one and the same disciplinary inquiry. The inquiry is just dragged like that and the officer/man under inquiry suffers the sufferings and victimization. Unless a period of time specifying the limitation is fixed, there may take place a lot of enforcement crimes just by causing undue delay in the completion of disciplinary cases. Some enforcement crimes in this area come from the nature of government jobs themselves as they are jobs in Government—but they are made worse by the culpable indifference and negligence of those who can in some cases, remedy them. In some instances, the disciplinary authorities take tolerant or lenient views towards certain people and that is the reason why one and the same act becomes a misconduct depending upon the person who commits it. Late arrivals become a misconduct in the case of some people whereas they are not so in the cases of some others. Why? The subordinates see such differential treatment and naturally, they resent them. Their resentments may be the cause of further enforcement crimes.

'Public interest'—what does it mean in disciplinary matters? Just go through the charge-memos issued. Then one may see the grounds of action. Sometimes, the charges may be vague. They may not be clear, precise, self-contained and accurate with date, time and place. They may not have a full and clear statement of allegation in support of each charge and the evidence upon which such charge is/charges are based. What is the public interest here? See the judgements from the courts.

* The charge-sheet and the statement of allegations furnished to the petitioner clearly showed that the disciplinary authority started with the assumption that the petitioner was guilty of the charges framed against him and that even before an enquiry was conducted it was assumed that the charges were proved against him. The punishment which was proposed to be imposed upon the petitioner was also specified in the charge—sheet.[19]

* The inspector general of police in his letter addressed to the subordinate officer requested to deal with the sub-inspector of police and punish him for misconduct and report compliance. It cannot be said that the conclusions reached against petitioner have been reached without the person holding the inquiry being influenced by the direction of the inspector general of police.[20]

If public interest is what is intended, then there is no scope for any prejudices, bias or preconceived notions. Disciplinary inquiries are conducted not to satisfy the personal interest or to express one's bias against the officer/man under inquiry. Why does this occur? How does such a situation come about? The culture that exists in government service is such that the disciplinary authority can express its bias and prejudices to trouble a subordinate and in so doing, there is no harm for the disciplinary authority. The officer/man under inquiry carries his cross and the disciplinary authority may watch and enjoy such traumatic experiences to which the officer/man under inquiry is exposed. An impartial man to such biased inquiries can see that the disciplinary authority then behaves like an ethical moron or imbecile. Such authority does not understand the purpose of public interest and the meaning of disciplinary inquiries. In such situations, the officer/man under inquiry is often left alone with his problems and victimization. There may be situations of acute poverty, anxiety and frustration for the officer/man under inquiry. He may suffer the unbearable pain even to see his both ends meet, so much so, that the victims of enforcement crimes commit suicide. This may be the reason why the rules insist that the principles of natural justice must be fully respected during the conduct of disciplinary inquiries.

Presumptions and Enforcement Crimes

Presumptions taken in a disciplinary inquiry cause enforcement crimes. The general principles followed in disciplinary inquiries in police:

1. Disciplinary inquiries are "fact finding" inquiries.
2. They are conducted by administrative authorities.
3. Rigid standards of a criminal trial need not be applied in disciplinary inquiries.

I have asked many inquiring officers to tell me more details regarding "rigid standards of a criminal trial". Many officers belonging to armed reserve/batallions could not understand the question as they had little or no exposure to criminal trials. Yet, they functioned as "inquiry officers".

The guidelines further state that "it is not expected that the benefit of every reasonable doubt must necessarily go to accused officer. Where two possible views can be reasonably taken, it is the right and duty of the inquiry and disciplinary authorities to decide which is the view to be taken in the particular case". What does it mean? Words like "possible views" and "reasonably taken", etc, do not mean much—but lead to enforcement criminality. The guidelines say further: "Full weight must be given to the common course of natural events, human conduct and of public and private affairs. Where the conduct of the accused officer is found to be at variance with these, a presumption will be deemed to arise against the officer concerned". The guidelines are so confusing and vague that even a right minded inquiry officer/disciplinary authority may find it extremely difficult to proceed further without committing some enforcement crimes. There is a view that the rules governing disciplinary procedures are drafted in a manner that may cause confusion. The more one reads them, the more he may become confused, i.e., reading takes one from obscurities to obscurities and further to obscurities indeed!

The disciplinary authority is a very powerful authority. The punishments inflicted are very severe. In fact, the punishments which can be inflicted by a criminal court in some crimes may be fine which may be a few hundreds of rupees. But, the punishments inflicted by the disciplinary authority may be dismissal, removal, compulsory retirement, etc. In cases increments are stopped with cumulative effect, the amount may be several thousands. Precisely therefore, the inquiry must be conducted and decision must be taken with full justness and honesty.

* The inquiry officer acquitted the employee of two charges, but found him guilty of one charge. The disciplinary authority differed from the finding of inquiry officer and imposed a penalty for dismissal taking into account the charges on which the employee was acquitted, without giving a notice to the employee about his intention to differ from the findings of the inquiry officer. This was against all principles of fair play and natural justice.[21]

* When the penalty was imposed to withhold two increments with cumulative effect, it would indisputably mean that the two increments earned by the employee was cut off as a measure of penalty forever in his upward march of earning higher scale of pay. The insidious effect of the order is that the employee is

reduced in his time scale by two places and it is in perpetuity during the rest of his service with a direction that two years service would not be counted in his time scale of pay as a measure of penalty. The effect of this order is envisaged in Rule 5(v) of the Rules, i.e., "reduction to a scale stage in the time scale of pay for a specified period. It is a major penalty and imposition of the impugned penalty without inquiry is *per se* illegal.[22] In this case, the officer under inquiry had to approach the Supreme Court to get a decision in his favour. The disciplinary authority knows that many lower level functionaries may not be prepared to expend so much money, manpower and energy for the purpose. In fact, this works as a ground for enforcement crimes! The disciplinary authority has no accountability in such instances and the officer under inquiry has no right to get victimological compensation.

Hoarding of Files in Disciplinary Matters

In my book, *Crime and Society: Current Issues and Trends*, I have argued out that hoarding of files must be treated as a crime under law. In many disciplinary inquiries, no decision comes in time. It is delayed and dragged. When inquired into, no reply comes into, no reply comes in a proper way. There is no transparency. The officers/clerks who keep the file waste a lot of their energy and time in explaining "this and that" and not explaining anything worthy of any use for the officers under inquiry. Some officers/men under inquiry tell that the people who spend so much energy in explaining "this and that" can give consolation to them if they spend half of their energy in explaining the real facts. They do not speak the truth. They misguide people, supress facts, suggest falsehood and cause agony and anxiety. If what they say is true then they commit enforcement crimes to which the officers/men under inquiry are really helpless in the present state of affairs. All this explains, at least in part, how the value of life has deteriorated in disciplinary cases! There is widespread moral decline in disciplinary justice and this climate and culture mitigates the subjective responsibility of individuals who deal with disciplinary cases. In order to administer disciplinary justice, enormous sums of money are invested by the people and they continue to invest more. But, the end result is disappointing. There is a view that the government can save a lot of money if disciplinary actions are limited only to genuine cases. The various ways by which disciplinary cases are created, concocted, conducted and concluded must be monitored by just, honest and objective minds. Certainly, it will reduce the number of enforcement crimes in disciplinary areas and help to save a lot of money for the public exchequer.

All said and done, it is necessary that employees who exhibit misconducts are punished. Administration has to proceed further and it can go on only if the guilty are punished. What is required here is that there must be no scope for misusing the power conferred on the disciplinary authority and for committing enforcement crimes. People are proceeding towards an equal justice system in which justice is ensured to the delinquent, to the victims, victims of abuse of power/authority, society and to the legal system itself. Disciplinary legal system is a sub-system in the total system of Equal Justice Under Law.

References

1. *Sadasivan Pillai Vs. State of Kerala,* 1976 KLT 323.
2. *Delhi Electric Supply Undertaking Vs.G.P. Satsangi* 1984 Lab I C 54.
3. *N. C. Guchait Vs.D.M.,* 1966 IILLJ, 71 Cal.
4. *Veeramani Vs. State of Kerala,* 1974 KLT 630, O.P. Gupta Vs. Union of India, AIR, 1987 S C 2257.
5. *Satya Prakash Vs. Union of India,* 1980 (3) SLR 64.
6. *State of Uttar Pradesh Vs. Mohd. Nooh, AIR,* 1958 SC 86.
7. *Abdul Wajeed Vs. State of Karnataka,* 1981 (1) SLR 454.
8. *Kesavan Namboodiri Vs. State of Kerala,* 1982 KLT 512.
9. *K.R. Deb Vs. Collector, Central Excise, AIR,* 1971 SC 1447.

10. *Augustine Vs. Superintendent of Post Offices,* 1984 KLT 226.

11. *Bhagat Ram Vs. State of Himachal Pradesh,* (1983)2 SCC 442, AIR 1983 SC 454.

12. *Ramakant Misra Vs. State of Uttar Pradesh, AIR* 1982 SC 1552.

13. *Punnose Vs.Manager, P&T* 1977 (2) SLR 399.

14. *Zile Singh Vs.Sub Divisional Officer,* 1982 (2) SLR 225.

15. 1999 (1) KLT 313.

16. 1984, KLT 564.

17. *Senior Superintendent RMS Vs. Raghavan,* 1984 KLT 145.

18. AIR 1996 SC 484.

19. *KESHRE MAL VS. STATE OF RAJASTHAN,* 1979 (3) SLR 1.

20. *Kadar Vs. Deputy Superintendent of Police,* 1965 KLT 450.

21. *Narayana Misra Vs. State of Orissa,* 1969 (3) SLR, 657.

22. *Kulwant Singh Gill Vs. State of Punjab,* 1990 (6) SLR 73 SC.

7
MILLENNIUM POLICE AND JUSTICE

Today, at the conclusion of the second millennium or on the eve of the third millennium, policing and administration of justice via police face many challenges. The police and the people, therefore, must make a conscious and mature assessment of what the police do *hic et nunc* and to collect creative proposals for betterment. The police do have a tradition well established and widely practiced and therefore, it is appropriate or all the more necessary to make serious reflections on police performance in administration of just justice in the light of what is now called Equal Justice Under Law. Enforcement crimes have no place in administration of equal justice to all under law. This is otherwise called the 'distributive justice' to everyone under a system of justice—"All Rights to All Under the Sun".

Enforcement Crimes and Police Formation

In forming a police officer, police personality, the police training institutions play an important and vital role. Nevertheless, the significance of police training in the right perspective is not recognized even today in police service. Police performance of the duty is as the law wants them to do and not in the way the police want them to be done. In the former case, enforcement crimes have no scope whereas, in the latter case, they do have. Police training should bear in mind this golden rule in its various dimensions. After recruiting a raw person and before he is entrusted to perform his police duties, he is asked to set aside a period of time for training. The aim of training is to develop an understanding of what exactly is the role of police in a democracy and how should the duties be performed in a just and human rights friendly way—without violating the laws and without committing enforcement crimes. Respecting the laws which the police try to enforce in society means that they are administering justice to all. The people want the police to be the witnesses to what they want to enforce in society. In such a state of affairs, enforcement crimes do not take place. A police training centre is and must be, more than a place for giving police training to raw recruits, a place for human formation. It is certainly an atmosphere that fosters and ensures a process of formation so that a person who is recruited to police service may become a living image of law and law enforcement in a just manner. Somehow or other, police administration and people responsible for training and human formation forget it and the result is the commission of enforcement crimes in various ways and magnitudes while the police perform their duties. The models for the police functionaries must not suffer from personality defects or defective character traits. People who have proven records of character and conduct or are notoriously known for lack of integrity might become the directors/principles of police training institutions. The faculty too might be of the same nature or similar characteristics. Police training and human formation during the training period are responsibilities that people with character and upright conscience must reserve for themselves.

Aspects of Police Training

As a whole, one may say that the police training depends heavily on the quality of the candidates for police service as well as on the integrity and commitment of the trainers and the authenticity of the ideals in which they are trained. The general spectrum of police training must be as follows: during the time of police training, a police officer/man must pass from his wrong concepts/perceptions of police officer/man and his work to correct and acceptable concepts/perceptions. He must learn to perform his duties in a profound and intense way keeping in mind his obligations as a responsible police man/officer in a democracy. A police officer's/man's maturity in performing his duties and responsibilities may be reflected in permeating all the human and human rights elements in him including his emotional, physical, intellectual and administrative lives.

Why do enforcement crimes take place? There are three or more sets of people entering into police service. First, those who view police work as something possible for them to do and such people are found to be honest and sincere. Generally, they do not involve themselves in committing enforcement crimes. If they commit an enforcement crime, they experience guilt for it. Second, those who show hesitation and they doubt their genuine intentions in becoming a police officer/man. I have asked many trainees to be honestly frank about their intention in becoming police officers/men. I have noticed that there were a number of trainees who belonged to the second category and certainly I have seen that such people later becoming enforcement criminals. In due course, while they are in service, they become corrupt and accept money for any and many things. They commit enforcement crimes. Thirdly, those who do not have any attitude or aptitude for police job and they opt for police job because they did not get a better job or a job which opened opportunities to express authority/power or misuse/abuse of the authority or power for personal advantages. As a senior member on the faculty of a police training institution in India, I may emphatically say that careful inquiry must be made concerning the trainees' right intentions and freedom of choice, his physical, moral and intellectual fitness, adequate mental health, capacity for understanding the obligations of responsible policing and carrying out the police responsibilities in a befitting manner in a democracy. Dishearteningly enough, one wonders whether or not any attempt is made anywhere in India in this direction. I feel that there is regrettable shortage of right police officers/men in India and one of the main reasons is the unwillingness of the authorities to firmly implement reliable and objective tests to find out the right persons to do the right jobs in police work.

People who have a proneness to corruption-money must not be posted to perform field work through which they can make fortunes for themselves.

Human Formation in Police and Enforcement Crimes

'Human formation' is something about which the police hierarchy is not very much keen at present. The hierarchy is concerned with physical formation and intellectual formation and precisely therefore policemen/officers with human face do not come in large numbers. Gore Committee on police training spoke about human formation, but the recommendation did not capture adequate attention. Today, it is accepted that human formation is the basis of all police formations. The psychology of human needs, motivations, emotions, personal growth, etc, helps everyone understand the strength and frailty of a given mode of formation. Identity of an authentic human being must be there when one performs police job. The identity is not just a role one fulfills or a job one holds in justice administration. Identity is one's unique psychological make-up.

The youths seek ideals and so do the policemen/officers. Police must have the noblest of ideals and they must be given nothing less. Police officers who have the nicknames like leopard, tiger, lion, thunder, etc, should not be the models. During their identity formation—both inside the training institutions and outside—they must have good ideals. The police do not have such ideals today. They have in front of them, comfort seeking and corrupt officials who commit many types of enforcement crimes. They do not absorb values of enforcement justice. Unless policemen/officers do not absorb the values of enforcement justice, the entire exercise to have an enforcement crime-free police service will remain a mere pious wish.

The police officers/men must know the inner aspirations of the people and expectations of the society. They must know the depths of their responsible obligations and for it, they must be educated to love truth and justice-to be true and just to their words—to be genuinely justice conscious, to be men of integrity and particularly to be balanced in their judgement and behaviour. They must not be arrogant or quarrelsome, but affable, just, honest in their words and heart. They must be prudent and discrete, generous and ready to serve, capable of opening themselves to maintain enforcement justice in all activities.

The whole work of police training would be deprived of its necessary foundation if it lacked a suitable human formation. Every policeman/officer is the living image of justice and by that truth alone, he must seek to reflect in himself the human perfection which must be reflected in his attitude towards others—suspects, complainants, and so on. Every police officer/man who wants to avoid enforcement crimes must cultivate a series of human qualities, not only out of proper growth and realization of self, but also with a view to perform his duties and obligations as a police functionary. These qualities are needed for them to be balanced and to become just enforcement officers. They have to be strong and free in their activities and must be capable of bearing the weight of police responsibilities. The police now and especially during the 21st century must love the truth, be loyal, respect every person and his dignity, have a sense of justice, to be true to the words, etc. Police—the word—(Politeness, Obedience, Loyalty, Integrity, Courage and Efficiency)—means a lot in these days and during the days to come.

'Human formation' in police administration, as pointed out earlier, was not given a distinct emphasis in police till yesterday and even today. But, today the need is felt more as the criticism against the police is often centered around the behavioural aberrations and misconducts of police. Enforcement crimes are the manifestations of the lack of human formation in police service. Ever since, I joined the police service as a civilian member, I have been trying to give emphasis to human formation. I wrote many books relating to human behaviour. One sparrow cannot make a change in the season and therefore, my attempt hitherto has been successful, perhaps, to give a distinct place for human formation in police administration. I may even say that human formation must be placed even before any other formation in police service, because human formation is seen as the foundation of all police activities and the lack of it is the source of all kinds of enforcement crimes in the current law enforcement.

Discipline has a place in human formation. Discipline must be seen not in terms of giving smart salutes, responding "yes sir, no sir" to superior officers, adherence to rules and departmental instructions, etc, but in reference to human growth. However, this new dimension has not been insisted very much till yesterday. The rules, salutes 'yes sir, no sir' attitude, etc, must be for the proper growth in personality.

The growth stated above takes place or can take place only in an atmosphere of freedom. The freedom is certainly balanced with accountability. The police are free to do many things and commission of enforcement crimes is a misuse or abuse of the freedom. The police are accountable to their acts and one of the factors in accountability is authority. An authority without accountability is no authority at all.

When enforcement crimes are committed, the police misuse/abuse their authority. They do so because, they think that they are not accountable to what they do.Transparency is lacking in many enforcement crimes. Instead of becoming men of communication they become men of secretiveness and that is the reason why transparency is not seen in enforcement crimes.

The policemen/officers today are no more closed in their world of secretiveness, but living in society and closer to people than ever in the past. The police closeness to people and their life in visibility of the public lay many compulsions upon them. They will be, as a consequence, restrained to commit enforcement crimes as they used to be in the past. They have to avoid all sorts of enforcement crimes which alone will make them more acceptable to people.

Stability in character and ability to make carefully weighed decisions are two pre-requisites to avoid enforcement crimes. A sound judgement of issues and events, self-control, strength of character and self-esteem are necessary to ensure enforcement justice to people. Accountability, transparency, fidelity to promises, restraint, self-esteem, integrity, etc, too are essential. Courtesy including the use of proper language and respectful behaviour honouring human dignity are signs of maturity. A genuine search for the dominant values of the society and an earnest attempt to identify the core-values of police community are essential for any police officer/man who wants to become enforcement-crime free in society.

The trainers and superiors themselves, by their example, approachability, supervision in human rights friendly manner and availability, must be models. The hierarchy of police by their examples of their wholesome relationships with people, fellow colleagues, subordinates and superiors, with their acceptance of their own limitations and failures, should become living witnesses of what it means "human" in police life.

Formation in Enforcement Just Behaviour

Enforcement just life presupposes maturity in justice administration. This implies a proper awareness of one's own role and justice consciousness. There are three important points in assessing one's enforcement just maturity. The first is that the more mature a police officer/man is in his professional life, the more he will possess awareness about his limitations, failures, roles and justice consciousness. A mature police officer/man will be able to recognize and draw inferences from his official responses as they affect his interactions with others. The second is that his responses to the requirement of enforcement justice will be more than just conformity to a law. He will have to understand what he is doing and must be willing to accept what is right without bitterness. The more a police officer/man finds enforcement justice as an imposition, the more it will diminish his degree of maturity of justice consciousness. Thirdly, there must be a harmony among his thinking, speaking and acting in police life.

Everyday during the career in police, every police officer/man must continue discerning whether he has the gift of being just in his work. The challenges to justice administration must be placed before him in such a way that atleast he makes an explicit commitment for justice administration as a value and discipline in life. Enforcement just behaviour is always linked with other virtues in police life.

Physical Training and Enforcement Crimes

Till now somehow or other an idea had crept into police that for every policeman/officer, physical training is the core that unifies and gives life to his being a police officer/man and his acting as a police officer/man. Robust physique was considered as a *sine-qua-non* for success and efficiency in police work. Any amount of proof that physical fitness is not everything in police success could not convince the authorities and the hierarchy. They believed that police training would be left without foundation if excessive physical training was not given. Hence, an excessively high dose of physical training was given to police officers/men during the period of their induction course. Intellectual training was neglected and the overemphasis given to physical training in academies and police training institutions made intellectual training a neglected area. Academicians or experts qualified in police science, management, criminology, etc, were seldom appointed or if at all appointed were given only lower status in the hierarchy. If they were civilians, then they were separated from the executive ranks in police service. Whatever that be, even today, one may see that there is reluctance to accept the fact that intellectual training is more important than or as important as physical training for civil police. Overemphasis given to physical training, even after the recommendations to give only due importance to physical training by the Central Committee on police training, was, perhaps, the continuation of a traditional approach to police training. Performance of parade, drill, route marches, acquiring of a sort of presumed discipline or collective response to the words of command, internalizing blind obedience to superiors' orders, conquering of certain evils in interpersonnel relationships, a negative approach to human feelings in police work, etc, were considered to be more important than intellectual training. They are, no doubt, good in themselves, but they lack human approaches to issues, events and individuals. Above all, a police officer/man is an authentic human reality in the society with just and human rights friendly attitudes and approaches. A human familiarity with people, colleagues, superiors and subordinates is particularly and specifically important for meaningful and responsible policing. In physical training what is essentially needed is a human approach towards people of all categories and descriptions.

Human approach has an essential and undeniable justice dimension. The human approach and enforcement crime free policing must be essentially sealed by a missionary zeal and dynamism. Justice is nothing but intimacy with the Constitution of India and the laws enacted thereunder and the implementation of law in accordance with the procedure established by law matters a lot. Enforcement crime free policing is the expression of love towards justice and the law enforcement must be in the direction of what the people and society want it to be enforced. My life in police and my long experience in police service have confirmed my conviction that responsible policing alone is the soil which can nourish an effective police activity in a democracy. The enforcement crimes and the various ways they are committed today are rooted in the tradition which the British established in India. The British had only one interest in India—their rule—but the democratic India has many interests. Enforcement criminality might have been encouraged by the British, but is not so now by the Indian society. Today, the policemen/officers are trained (as the people want) in such a way that they are (ought to) initiated into the democracy's policing. Democracy's policing has many dimensions which are rooted in public opinion and their appreciation of police officer/man must be competent enough to think that "the police are the people and the people are the police". People want a man in every policeman. Only this can make the police officers/men to be men of enforcement crime free policing.

The intellectual training of police officers/men is based on the study of laws, rules, standing orders and the subjects given in the syllabi for the officers/men. Nevertheless, people are found to be reluctant to accept that the policemen/officers are intellectually well trained. Why? My studies on "why do people refuse to accept that the intellectual training given to police officers is really of a high standard", prove that the faculty taking classes in academies/training institutions have not proved their merit qualitatively before the people. For many, the condemned people go to police training institutions and as such they fail to get due recognition and appreciation for what they do.

As the dawn of third millennium is at arm's length, the police is being repeatedly requested to be more human, just and human rights friendly. Protection of Human Rights Act came into existence in 1993 and thereafter, the people are watching the police functions very closely. In a TV programme, a police officer said: "We proved the case without resorting to any third degree methods". The viewer of the TV programme then commented: "as if he did a great charity to humanity".

After the enactment of the Protection of Human Rights Act-1993, many police officers who were trained in the traditional methods of police investigation asked: "How to collect evidence and obtain confessions without the use of third degree?". Recently a journalist told me that a police officer asked him: "can you prove a crime without the use of force, coercion and third degree?" He told me further that many police officers still believed that torture was a part and parcel of their culture. "Yes, it was so for a police officer who believed in the traditional methods of crime investigation". It is high time that the methods are changed and a change in methods alone can ensure an enforcement crime-free society.

Human rights friendly approach is what the people and the

times want now. Hence, every policeman/officer must be human rights friendly. He must have a fundamental attitude to respect human person and his dignity. Policing a society is a task and a call which demands a free and committed response on the part of police functionaries. The essential content of responsible policing is crime—free society which means an enforcement crime—free police service as well. There may be a number of policemen/officers who offer such meritorious services and they alone must be the models. Only in offering enforcement crime free services to people, will policing become meaningful in a democracy. A distorted sense of policing is at work today. In evaluating the worth of police service, one cannot close his eyes towards what the police do to enforce justice or in the pretext of enforcing justice.

Wounded Policeman, Wounded Police Officer and Wounded People

Everyone is wounded and precisely therefore every one needs healing. People commit crimes and the police deal with crimes and criminals. In dealing with crimes and criminals, police too commit crimes and that is the real problem today. Policemen (constables) do not enjoy high status even today. People fear the police and the fear of police is getting diminished day by day owing to increased public awareness of police powers and limitations. Many people in society are far superior in knowledge and education than the educated police constables and officers including those in the Indian Police Service. They think and say: "A policeman is not his own. He does not exist for himself, but for the people and the society". But, often one sees that the policeman/officer exists primarily for himself and some of them make a luxurious living by and through the jobs they do for the people and the society. How?

Such self-serving police personnel may not have any justice consciousness. Resultantly, wounded people suffer all sorts of enforcement injustice. There may exist a gap between what is in law and what is seen in practice. Why? The answer may be that the policemen/officers too are wounded and there is no healing for their wounds. Pressures on police, political interference, frequent transfers, low salary, no status, heavy work load, no promotions, depression, disciplinary actions, etc, may be responsible for the commission of enforcement crimes. No doubt, the policemen and officers are wounded. Does it mean that the people too must be wounded by becoming victims of enforcement crimes by police functionaries?

Enforcement Crimes and Credibility Crisis

I asked a question to many people and wanted them to answer: "How do you evaluate the policemen/officers today?" (1999). The responses were many and I enumerate here only those responses which are related to enforcement crimes:

1. They are corrupt
2. They are justice unfriendly
3. They concoct evidence
4. They create witnesses
5. They ignore the poor and downtrodden
6. They are susceptible to influence
7. They suffer from low self-esteem and thus one can list out more than 90 responses against the police—and relating to the commission of enforcement crimes in police work.

What is most disconcerting to me is the fact that loss of credibility seems most severe with regard to basic human qualities. People become disillusioned and the policemen/officers do not seem to have taken note of this(?) Criticisms against police functionaries in the press, media, films, TV serials, street corner meetings, legislatures, research studies are often dismissed by the police as anti-police approach of people having vested interests. What a tragedy indeed!

"Enforcement crimes"—this is a new concept introduced by

me to criminology. I understand that a police service which is enforcement crime-free is indeed a police service which is people friendly. I wanted to know the expectations of people with regard to the person of a police officer/man and the services he renders to the people. What kind of person a policeman/officer ought to be? And what kind of services he ought to perform? I asked these questions to many people in society and roughly I can say—

The Ideal Policeman/oficer

* Many visitors to police stations want the police to be more receptive.
* Many complainants to police say that they must be more listening.
* Many petitioners to police want the police to be more honest in the disposal of petitions.
* Many witnesses in criminal cases say that the police must be more considerate to them.
* Many suspects to police stations express their view that the police ought to be more human rights friendly (*More than 50 per cent).

Thus, one may notice that all categories of people who approach the police have dissatisfaction—high or low. Perhaps, they may say the same if they are asked to evaluate the officers/men in other Government departments. Many people, irrespective of their status (as witnesses, suspects) are in agreement that the policemen/officers need to change in their behaviour. Do the changes in behaviour come under the category of enforcement crimes? Certainly, some are. Enforcement crimes may be unknown to the people, yet they speak out that something is lacking in police subculture. People's expectations are very high and if the police are not able to satisfy the public, certainly it may have bearing on the erosion of credibility of police functionaries.

Police have to be faithful to the laws they enforce and the

khakhi uniform is not a licence to involve themselves in the commission of enforcement crimes. Police have to promote the feelings of security/safety among the people. They must ensure happiness to them. Enforcement crimes do not offer both and as such there occurs credibility crisis. There are different, even conflicting, expectations among various people who approach the police for services.

What kind of service the policemen/officers must perform? The responses from the people show that the most important function of police is delivering justice to the people. The police may say that prevention of crime is the most important function. This may be what the police Acts insist the Police to do. This traditional duty of police may not be acceptable to the people. For, prevention of crime in an unjust way—through commission of enforcement crimes—may not succeed in creating public credibility on police functions. What sort of a person the policeman/officer must be is more important than what duties he performs in society.

Do the perceptions of the people about policemen/officers match with their expectations? Do the people find in the police the qualities they expect in them? Do they see the police performing their functions in the way they expect them to perform? With regard to the functions of policemen/officers, the perceptions do not match people's expectations. With regard to the qualities expected in police functionaries, there exists a big gap between expectations and perceptions. The qualities which the people value most in police—officers/men are perceived to be lacking in many. Enforcement crime-free policing is generally deemed to be the most important quality of a police officer/man. I think that this is a matter which deserves serious concern. For people, what is most important is the quality of police work and not their professional success in an unacceptable manner. With a low level of credibility, the police cannot provide justice to the people.

Almost all police officers/men rendering service today are born after India became independent. If at all some are not, all have joined the police after independence. Law enforcement via commission of enforcement crimes might have been the style of British police in India. Democracy's police could very well avoid imperialist methods. Whatever that be, during the 1970's, the recommendations of Gore Committee came into being. After 1975 the police training was given in the way the Central Committee (Gore) had recommended. Even today, the same is followed. Police officers/men trained after 1975 work with those who were trained earlier. Hence, I wanted to know how did the older police officers/men render their services? The younger officers/men are trained according to new orientation signalled by Gore Committee. Are the new generations of police officers/men more credible and acceptable than the older ones? I asked this question to the people and many stated that the younger police officers/men were superior to the older ones in their behaviour. This shows that the credibility crisis was more serious for the older policemen/officers than the younger ones. In other words, the credibility gap is narrowing and is not widening now. This may be due to several factors like increased accountability, transparency, etc, in police work.

The government of this country spend a lot of money on police. After investing so much money, police service appears to fail to deliver goods—atleast quality goods—in an enforcement crime free manner? The police officers/men are ill-equipped to exercise their powers in an acceptable manner to the people? They fail to earn the trust and respect of the people they serve? These questions are asked not only by the people seated on high pedestals, but also the ordinary man on the street and the policemen themselves. Police men claim that, they are in society to administer justice in an enforcement crime free manner, but I do not know whether or not the people too may accept the police in *toto* or in part. In any case, the argument in third millennium will witness a justice system that may be called "Equal Justice System" which is intended to offer distributive justice.

Third Millenium and Equal Justice Under Law

In many of my books, I have elaborately and extensively dealt with what I mean by Equal Justice System and I do not think that I must repeat the same here. Third millennium will certainly witness an Equal Justice System and the police will become a part of that system. Justice is quantified and every man/woman wants to get his/her share of justice whenever crime takes place in society. The police will be forced to offer distributive justice to people in an enforcement crime free manner.

Man is created with potency to commit crimes and certainly he will continue to commit crimes. If that is a reality, the police or some other organised service agencies will have to deal with it—not alone, but along witn people and only with public participation in the years to come. Gone are the days that the police can any longer claim that they are to prevent and investigate crimes. I do not think that the people are going to accept that or what is enumerated in Police Acts as the duties of police. People today demand that the police are to administer equal justice. Once—just recently—an engineering student registered an FIR in a police station for the loss of his watch whose purchase value was Rs 450 or a little above. He spent some money to accelerate the investigation and after a few days, he wished to withdraw his case as he found that the continued investigation meant more money from his pocket that too without any hope of recovering the lost watch. He wanted justice and therefore he insisted that the investigation ought to be stopped at that stage, for, he thought that the stopping of investigation would be the proper justice then for him.

Today people want criminal justice and the police must do everything possible towards that end in a human rights friendly way—in an enforcement crime free manner. People have seen how the police behaved till now to the crime doers and they have also seen the acquittal and conviction rates. They have seen how the police investigated criminal cases and how they managed to get convictions. Enough is enough and now they demand that the police need to behave in a human rights friendly manner—in an enforcement crime free manner—so that the crime-doers are ensured justice. People weigh the advantages and disadvantages of human rights friendly-unfriendly behaviour by police. In their wisdom and out of their experience, the people think and endorse the view that human rights friendly police are always better than human rights unfriendly police. They do not want the police to commit enforcement crimes to investigate or prevent crimes. Hence, criminal justice in an enforcement crime free environment is what is expected from police in these days.

Victims of justice or victims of crime want victim justice first before anything is done to administer criminal justice. Instances are plenty to show that the victims are pressured to spend money from their pockets (e.g. to provide fuel for police vehicles) to conduct investigation or to speed up the works connected with investigation of crime. The victims of crime may do anything untill they have the hope that the crime will be investigated properly and the criminal may be detected. If the police cannot detect the criminal or the detected criminal escapes punishment then the victims of crime feel sorry for what they have done earlier to *speed up* the investigation. They feel that injustice has been committed to them.

Today, in theft, pock-pocketing or offences in which money is lost by the victims of crime, they want somehow or other to recover their lost money, even if it is less, and some of them do not want to prefer a FIR for conducting an investigation. A retired superintendent of police lost his car stereo which was insured against loss. He went to a police station and told the station house officer: "I lost my car stereo. You may register a case or do anything. I want to file papers before the insurance company to claim the loss". I asked him: "why do you take such an approach ?". He told me that he was not very keen to see that the thief was punished. At the same time, he was very particular to see that he recovered his loss. In motor vehicle accidents, the victims of accidents and their dependents are found to be interested to get the MACT claim more than punishing the rash and negligent drivers. If the drivers are punished, it is O.K., even otherwise, it is O.K. provided they do get maximum MACT claims. Some victims of traffic accidents are prepared to compromise with the drivers provided they jointly try to get maximum MACT claims. Even in rape cases, proposals are sent to enact laws so that the victims get compensation for their loss, irrespective of the fact that the rapist is punished after a trial. As it is, many rapists are not punished, so much so, that the people are not having trust on the machinery that the culprit will be punished. Proposals are also there to fix a time-frame for completion of investigation in rape cases. As it is, the trend is to see that victim justice is ensured more than criminal justice is administered by a prolonged investigation and trial of criminal cases. People now propose to have a victim fund for administering victim justice in criminal cases. This means that criminal justice along with victim justice is what the people desire now.

Even in administering victim justice, people do not want to see that the crime-doers are made victims of abuse of power and misuse of authority by the law enforcement agencies. The argument is that victims of the abuse of power and misuse of authority must have an actionable claim for getting victim compensation, if they are subjected to enforcement crimes by police or other agencies. Victim justice administration in an enforcement crime free atmosphere is what is favoured by the people and international community. This is what is called distributive justice, i.e., justice being distributed to the crime-doers and victims of crime/victims of abuse of power and authority under an equal justice system. The approach is extended to include even the dependents of crime-doers in case the crime-doers are seen to be the victims of enforcement crimes.

What is justice to the society? Society which spends enormous amount of money to maintain the justice system expects criminal justice as well as victim justice. As they are today, many criminals are not detected or if at all detected, then they are not punished by courts of law after the trial of the cases. As far as the victims of crimes are concerned, many victims do not get justice either psychologically or otherwise. Earlier, the society thought that action against the crime and the punishment afterwards offered victim satisfaction in a psychological way. As more and more criminals escape detection and conviction, the psychological satisfaction is not ensured. Hence, the victims of crime/victims of abuse of power and authority want victim justice. The justice to society now means justice to criminal and victims done in an enforcement crime free manner. The input invested by the society to the legal system must pay rich dividends by way of output and the third millennium marches towards such a justice under an equal justice system which distributes justice to all concerned with or affected by the commission of crimes.

Equal Justice System envisages a just justice system and it includes administration of justice by the sub-systems operating within the legal system as well as the whole system of justice administration. There is a thinking that justice is what the judge thinks. This thinking is now questioned as the society feels that justice is what the people want. As pointed out earlier, the rule of law is not what is required now, rather it is the rule of justice that is in demand at present. The society wants an enforcement crime free rule of law and does not favour a crude enforcement of the rule of law. That is the precise reason why the society insists human rights justice, gender justice, victim justice, social justice, just justice, juvenile justice, etc, to be absolutely honoured by the legal system. Then only, the justice administration can claim that the system is ensuring justice to the system itself. Delay in investigation, prosecution, trial, frequent adjournments, prolonged stay in prisons as undertrial prisoners, illegal detentions in police custodial facility, unauthorized methods of interrogating, harassment in court procedures, increased rate of acquittals, ego-clashes among the sub-systems in justice administration, indifferent conduct of criminal cases, excessive expenditure involved in obtaining justice, etc, are infamies to the justice system and injustice to the society.

Third millennium is marching towards an equal justice system which, I have discussed in detail in my earlier books[1], ensures justice to the crime-doers, to the victims of crime, victims of abuse of power and authority, to the society and to the legal system itself. Enforcement crimes defeat the very purpose of an equal justice system and are treated as a supreme dishonour shown to people's wish for a rule of justice in the years to come.

Reference

1. James Vadackumchery, *Third Millennium Police: Take off Trends in India,* A.P.H. Publishing Corporation, Delhi, 1999 and *Indian Police and Equal Justice Under Law,* A.P.H. Publishing Corporation, Delhi, 1999.

8

AN EPILOGUE: A WORD MORE ON ENFORCEMENT CRIMES

Enforcement crimes I hope will receive more attention in the years to come. They have to. For everything the police do has a person at the receving end. He is not an object but a 'human person' with dignity. But objectification has been in vogue in police sub-culture wherein the police enforced the law, but only with a partial appreciation of the human reality behind the law enforcement. That might be the reason why torture, harassment, humiliation, human rights violation, corruption, etc, could be noticed in police sub-culture.

What is the police role in a democracy? The essence of police role, many think, is performing duties as per law. But how?—By any means?—Through any methods? No. The essence of police role consists in performing police duties as per law and procedure established by law with a social dimension. This is called the meaningful existence of police service and certainly, such a service is purposive. The purpose will never be the commission of enforcement crimes. I cannot agree with people or institutions which say that torture has been institutionalized in Indian police. For torture is not and cannot be the species character of any police service anywhere in the world. Torture is doubtlessly an enforcement crime and had torture been the species character of the police in India, they would not have survived for 50 years after India became independent. Police had a lot of plus points, but they were not projected out as they ought to have been. Only the negative points were projected out and highlighted by many including the media, politicians, courts, commissions, etc, with the result that the police-caricature has been far away from being satisfactory. People thought and said that there has been no 'I-Thou' relationship between the police and the people. The relationship that existed has been only 'I-It' relationship between police and the people. Objectification, was at the root of this 'I-It' relationship. The British, probably, wanted only such a relationship and the training they imparted to police and which the Indian police followed after independence too was such that the police could not see the human face of the people at the receiving end. Police, it was alleged, had only a sort of animated human activities as they thought that the essence of police work was enforcing the law only, and nothing more. Law must be executed not by the police alone, but along with the people and both the police and the people must have the feeling of a "togetherness" when they do so. In such a system, enforcement crimes have little or no scope. What was lacking in India till now was the "Communication" between the police and the man or vice versa. As a result, the I-Thou relationship was missing altogether. Incidently, the police officers who thought that the police was a Force and not a Service believed that muscle *power* was the greatest power and with that power, they could achieve everything in law enforcement. Human existence and its meaning to police service to people were unknown to many police functionaries till recently, perhaps until the passing of the Protection of Human Rights Act-1993. Till then, some or almost all police officers/men sincerely thought that the police force was made up of *lathies*, hand-cuffs, rifles, human muscles, cruel faces, authority and pseudo authority, etc, and they honestly believed that they were the tools for law enforcement, crime investigation, prevention of crimes and other activities connected with police work. The Tool Existence of police kept the people away from the police. The police used their tools to handle people and certainly, in such a tool existence, there could be no human touch. The police touched the tools to manage and manipulate people. *Lathies* touched the people, muscles manipulated the people, cruel faces and harsh looks managed police-public interactions. But, in human existence, police comes closer to people and this proximity brings forth the togetherness—the communion—the I-Thou relationship between policeman and man. In human existence, there will be concern for others and wherever, one sees the caring concern, necessarily, there will not be any enforcement crimes.

The governments which came into power from time to time tried to use the police as tools to protect their political interests as a coercive weapon to subdue the people. The result has been that the police had only a sort of tool relationship with the people and there has been no human relationship. The police could not realize that they were distancing themselves from the people. They failed to understand that their interaction has been with people who have human existence. The police being a tool of the government thought that they were dealing with people who were also the tools. In due course, many say, politicians, the affluents, the social higher ups and the influential made attempts to use police as tools for achieving their vested interests. This tool-approach had its impact on many enforcement crimes which the police committed. The *neta* (the leader), the *babu* (the bureaucrat), the *dalal* (the agent or go between) and the *dada* (the *goonda*) thus made use of police as tools. All of them worked in, togetherness, in Communion in an I-Thou relationship with the police and thus made the people as objects through objectification.

Police in Itself, Police for Itself, Police for Others

Police in itself has no meaning in a democracy. Today's police experiences all the problems which any society has, from time immemorial, experienced. Even before organized policing came into existence, people were managing their problems in many ways. The society created the police not for itself but for the society. Police may do many things for itself and when it does so it becomes an enforcement crime. For example, the police investigates a crime and if it does, it for itself, it may resort to even foul means to achieve the goals. On the other hand, if it does the work for others, it cannot and will not commit any foul things. When police does anything for itself, it considers others as nothing or as having only a vegitative existence. This approach is objected to by the people in a democracy and that is the reason why the police becomes targets of public criticisms. The police are then called enforcement criminals. Police must be conscious of their social responsibilities. Of course there are laws which the police must enforce. But, every law has a conscience and whenever a policeman enforces the law without having a conscience, then he becomes just an animated policeman. He acts for others and the police in their corporate capacity does everything which a member in the society does. Police do not *lathi*-charge people because they have *lathies* with them, but they do so because the people want them to do so for their sake. There exists a fundamental relationship between the man and the policeman, and the relationship is a relationship of participation for a common good. There is no question of the policeman overmastering the man as the man is not a mere thing.

"We are the police and we are above grammar" approach without looking at the society and social needs may cause a number of enforcement crimes. The police must see the people in front of them, people whom they must scan objectively. "We are observing people"—this thought must be their reminder everyday. Any action without such a thought will not be rational or justifiable. Police are accountable. Human reality is of paramount importance in police actions. Acceptance of human reality is an acceptance of human relations between police and the people. It is an acceptance of I-Thou relationship in human transactions. The petitioner, the informant, the witnesses, the suspects, the visitors and all those who interact with police expect such an 'I-Thou' relationship. In such a relationship, exercise of pseudo-authority has no scope. There will not be any room for misuse of power or abuse of authority. The "human I" and the "human thou" must interact with each other. In such an interaction, inflated egos play no role and eventually, the police become acceptable to all in society.

Man and Policeman

Every policeman has a man in him and every man has a policeman in him. If the man in policeman behaves, there will not be enforcement crimes. The man in policeman is a searcher of just justice, equal justice and such a man has values in him. Such a man values human person and his dignity.

Who is a policeman or better the policeman in man? This has to be understood from what the word means to people. A meaning is assigned to a word over a period and the policeman to Indians means some one to be afraid of and certainly people keep away from policemen as they are afraid of them. The distance which people keep from the police make them to commit more and more enforcement crimes. The more distance the people maintain from police, the less transparent the police become. This is a facilitating environment for the police to involve themselves in the commission of more and more enforcement crimes. Bringing people closer to police is a method of arresting enforcement crimes. How? The gap between man and policeman must be filled up by human elements, human contents, human person, human values, human existence, human essence and anything that may be human in human transactions. This book hopes to achieve this purpose.

Bibliography

Asch, Sidney, (1971), *Police Authority and Rights of the Individual,* Arco Publishing Company Inc., New York.

Bakhsis, Singh (1976), *The Supreme Court of India as an Instrument of Social* Justice, Sterling, New Delhi.

Baxi, Upendra (1982), *The Crisis of the Indian Legal System,* Vikas, Delhi.

Bayley, D.H., (1978), *Police and Political Development in India,* Princeton University Press.

Blumberg, A., (1967), *Criminal Justice,* Quadrangle Books, Chicago.

Cambliss, William, (1969), *Crime and Legal Process,* Mc Graw Hill Books, New York.

Carlin, Jerome, (1966), *Lawyer's Ethics,* Russel Sage, New York.

Davis, Kenneth, C., (1969), *Discretionary Justice,* Baton Rouge Lovistana State University Press.

Desai, A.R. (ed.) (1985), *Human Rights Violations in India,* Popular, Bombay.

Dhagamvar, Vasubha, (1974), *Law, Power and Justice,* N.M. Tripathi, Bombay.

Felkenes, George T., (1974), *The Criminal Justice System: Its Functions and Personnel,* Prentice Hall, Englewood, New Jersey.

Hart, H.L.A., (1971), *Law, Liberty and Morality,* Stanford University Press, California.

Iyer, Krishna, V.R., (1974), *Social Mission of Law,* Orient Longman, New Delhi.

Kriplani, J.B., (1977), Our Police During the Emergency, *Indian Express,* May 31.

Krishnamurthy, S., (1994), *Human Rights and Indian Police,* R.R.Publishers, Bangalore.

Lawrence, Friendman, (1975), *The Legal System,* Russel Sage Foundation, New York.

Macklin, Fleming, (1974), *The Prince of Perfect Justice,* Basic Books Ins., New York.

Misra, S.C., (1970), *Police Administration in India,* National Police Academy, Mount Abu.

Naik, V.V., (1970), Police Plans to Serve, National Police Academy, Magazine, November, 1970.

Nath, Trilok, (1978), *The Indian Police,* Sterling, Delhi.

Noorani, A.G., (1976), Police Excesses: Need For Institutional Safeguards, *Indian Express,* March 9.

Packer, H.L., The Police and The Community, *Stanford Law Review,* Vol. 22, 1314—17.

Rajan, V.N., (1983), *Whither Criminal Justice Policy,* Sagar Publications, New Delhi.

Report of the National Police Commission, Government of India, New Delhi.

Sen, Sankar and A.K.Saxena, (1994), *Police Training Problems and Perspectives,* Rawat Publications, New Delhi.

Sharma, P.D., (1981), *Police Polity and People in India,* Uppal Publishing House, New Delhi.

Sikra, Melvin, (1975), *The Administration of Injustice,* Harper and Row, New York.

Simpson, A.K. (1977), *The Literature of Police Corruption,* John Jay Press, New York.

Singhvi, G.C., *Police Administration vis-a-vis the Police Act of 1861: An Overview,* Police Research and Development, 4, Oct., 1975.

Subramonian, S., (1992), Human Rights and Police, Association For Advancement of Police and Security Sciences, Hyderabad.

Vadackumchery James (1999), *Police Leadership: The Inside Story,* A.P.H. Publishing Corporation, New Delhi.

Vadackumchery James, (1998), *Indian Police: 2001—What Went Wrong Here?,* A.P.H.Publishing Corporation, Delhi.

Venkatasubbarao, G.C., (1974), *Jurisprudence and Legal Theory.* Eastern Book, Lucknow.

Verghese, B.G., (1977), Our Police During the Emergency, *Indian Express*, May 31.

Wilson, James, (1975), *Thinking About Crime,* Basic Books, New York.

Wrsekar, H.S., (1973), *Law and Social Welfare,* Lalvani Publication, Bombay.

Index